COUNSELED BY GOD

How to Have a Quiet Time that Awakens Life Change

COUNSELED BY GOD

INVITING GOD TO COUNSEL AND TRANSFORM YOU THROUGH HIS WORD

DAVID N. JOHNSON
& J. A. JOHNSON

www.genesiscollegeandseminary.com

Counseled by God

Cover Designer: J. Martin

Editor: Paul Miller

Aneko Press

www.anekopress.com

Aneko Press, Life Sentence Publishing, and our logos are trademarks of

Life Sentence Publishing, Inc.
203 E. Birch Street
P.O. Box 652
Abbotsford, WI 54405

RELIGION / Christian Living / Spiritual Growth

Paperback ISBN: 979-8-88936-580-8

eBook ISBN: 979-8-88936-581-5

10 9 8 7 6 5 4 3 2 1

Available where books are sold

To my family: You are among God's sweetest gifts in my life. The Lord has used you to fill my days with joy, laughter, and purpose, and to remind me daily of His grace. I thank Him continually for each of you, and I pray that our lives together will always reflect His goodness and bring Him glory.

—David N. Johnson

To my Genesis Crew – Brian, Polito, Josh, Matt, and George: You have brightened my life with your friendship and your faithfulness to the proclamation of the gospel. I am forever indebted to you.

—J. A. Johnson

Your testimonies are my delight;
they are my counselors.
—Psalm 119:14

Table of Contents

Introduction

Counseled by God is a call to discover that the most faithful Counselor you could ever have is not a professional, a pastor, or even a best friend; it is the living God Himself, speaking through His Word.

Too many Christians settle for secondhand spirituality. They rely on their pastors to feed them once a week, expecting Sunday sermons to carry them through the challenges of Monday through Saturday. But spiritual nourishment is not meant to come on Sundays alone. It is meant to come daily, from the hand of God Himself.

This book will introduce you to a spiritual discipline that I (J.A.J.) have used for many years in my "quiet time," the time I set aside for personal devotions. This practice is called the GRIP method of Bible journaling, and it is designed to help you hear the living voice of God through His written Word.

In *Your Preaching Matters* (Aneko Press, 2025), I mention that GRIP journaling has been a tool to help me experience life transformation. It has not only served to help me hear the voice of God, but has also served as a way to record His dealings with me as He chips away my rough edges.

We wrote *Counseled by God* to elaborate on how the GRIP journaling method can serve as a conduit of grace to help believers grow in godliness and become more like Christ. The GRIP method consists of writing a journal entry with four sections:

G – God's Word: You read the Bible and write down a verse or a summary of verses that spoke to your heart. I encourage readers not to flippantly select passages each day but to read from a daily, systematic reading plan (like the ones provided in Resources 3 to 7).

R – Revelation: You record what God reveals to you about Himself, His purpose, His will, His nature, or yourself. God speaks through His Word, and this is where you write down what He is saying.

I – Implementation: You write how you will implement this truth into your life. Many believers hear what God speaks, but they do not do anything about it. In this section of your journal entry, you describe how you will specifically apply what God has spoken to your heart.

P – Prayer: You respond in prayer, sealing your time with God in personal worship. The prayer relates to what God spoke. It might be a confession, a commitment to obey what God revealed, or a prayer of thanksgiving and praise.

My introduction to spiritual journaling came through a method I learned from Wayne Cordeiro, the founding pastor of New Hope Christian Fellowship in Hawaii. During a leadership practicum he led on the beautiful island of Oahu, he introduced me and the other participants to SOAP – an acronym for Scripture, Observation, Application, and Prayer – as a practical framework for the daily study of God's Word. I embraced this method for several years, and it became the seedbed for what eventually grew into the GRIP method.

SOAP served me well, but I found that to truly get a "grip" on God's Word, we must go beyond simply observing what the Bible says. We must press deeper – discerning what God is revealing about Himself and about ourselves, allowing His Word to renew our minds, confront our comfort, conform us to the image of Christ, transform our character, and equip us for fruitful ministry. That desire for a richer, more transformative encounter with Scripture gave birth to GRIP, which has become an invaluable tool for deepening my intimacy with Christ and strengthening my walk with Him. I remain grateful to Dr. Cordeiro for awakening in me a passion for daily journaling as a discipline of spiritual growth.

What You Will Find Here

Counseled by God includes two parts. In Part 1, you will learn how to hear God through Scripture, structure your quiet time, and journal in a way that changes your life. In a world full of distractions and shallow interactions with the Bible, GRIP will teach you to slow down and connect deeply with God.

This is critical because spiritual transformation

does not happen by accident. We are not changed by occasional Bible verses or random devotionals. Transformation happens when we cultivate intentional habits of hearing from God and obeying His voice.

In Part 2, you will learn how GRIP also serves as a ministry tool. You will see how it can aid in sermon preparation, counseling conversations, and mentoring relationships. Those who have been counseled by God are best equipped to counsel others in truth and grace.

Finally, several resources are provided to help you cultivate lasting spiritual growth, including a start-up guide for using GRIP, sample journal entries, and Bible reading plans.

This book is for every believer – pastors and leaders, parents and teachers, counselors and laypeople, new believers and mature disciples. No matter your season of life or level of spiritual maturity, we all stand in daily need of God's counsel. And the good news is that He has made it abundantly available to us in His Word.

We pray that GRIP will help you in your quest to be conformed to the image of Christ. It is vital to hear Him speak every day. If you are not listening for His voice daily, you're missing out on the counsel He wants to give you. You're missing out on direction, guidance, healing, deliverance, encouragement, and wisdom. You're missing out on the words of life.

You were meant to live with clarity, power, and peace. May God's Word come alive to you as you apply what He reveals and learn to keep a tight GRIP on the Word that never fails.

Part 1

Introducing GRIP: A Journaling Tool to Hear God

Word of God functions as an ever-present, ever-reliable counselor for those who love Him. It does not just inform the mind, but it transforms the heart.

Author and professor Kelly Kapic, in his *A Little Book for New Theologians*, wrote:

> God's counsel and plans are known through the received oracles of God. . . . God teaches us through his revealed and recorded Word. Whether we rise or lie down, are home or in a foreign land, God's Word serves as the lamp to our feet and the light for our path (Psalm 119:105). Without it we remain in the dark and in desperate need. . . . These revealed words are to be cherished, both because of their divine origin as well as because of their transformative powers.[1]

God counsels us through His Word, and He speaks to us as no human can.

The Word Penetrates the Heart

Hebrews 4:12 declares, *For the word of God is living and active, sharper than any two-edged sword, piercing to the division of soul and of spirit, of joints and of marrow, and discerning the thoughts and intentions of the heart.* God's counsel is not shallow. It does not deal

1 Kelly M. Kapic, *A Little Book for New Theologians* (Downers Grove, IL: IVP Academic, 2012), 115-116.

with symptoms. It penetrates to the root. His Word diagnoses our true condition and exposes the hidden motives we ourselves may not even recognize.

Whereas worldly counsel aims to guide us, Scripture aims to sanctify us. It shows us where we've gone astray – not to shame us, but to rescue us. It offers correction – not to condemn, but to restore. God's counsel through His Word is like a scalpel in the hands of a skilled surgeon. It is painful at times, but it is always precise and healing.

A person may come to Scripture hoping to find comfort in hardship, only to discover that God first wants to address the pride in their heart. Another person may seek peace for a troubled relationship and find themselves being taught about the necessity of forgiveness. This is divine counsel at its finest – not merely answering our questions, but addressing the root causes of our problems.

To be clear, God *does* comfort and strengthen us. It is His nature to do so. He said, *I am he who comforts you* (Isaiah 51:12). The psalmist received such solace through Scripture: *This is my comfort in my affliction, that your promise gives me life* (Psalm 119:50). But God is more interested in our holiness than our happiness. His ultimate goal for us is not to be happy, but to be conformed to the image of His Son (Romans 8:29), becoming more like Him each day as we submit to His will.

As we consistently read and study God's Word, the hidden parts of our lives are examined – those secret places in our hearts that are not submitted to Christ.

Lustful thoughts, selfish motives, unforgiveness, and the desire for revenge are some of the unseen sins that reside deep within.

When we seek to be counseled by God through His Word, He exposes these areas of brokenness – teaching us, rebuking us, correcting us, and training us in righteousness so that *the man of God may be complete, equipped for every good work* (2 Timothy 3:16-17).

As we become complete, we become content. When we hunger and thirst for righteousness, we will be satisfied in God (Matthew 5:6).

The Role of the Holy Spirit

It is important to understand that the Word of God does not operate in isolation. God has given us the Holy Spirit, who illuminates the truth of Scripture and applies it to our lives. Jesus said in John 14:26, *The Helper, the Holy Spirit, whom the Father will send in my name, he will teach you all things and bring to your remembrance all that I have said to you.* Without the Spirit, we may read the Bible and miss the voice of God entirely. With the Spirit, however, we not only understand the words, but we receive them as personal, divine counsel.

The Spirit makes the Word alive to us. He convicts our hearts and affirms truth. He highlights specific passages at just the right time. Have you ever opened your Bible and found a verse that seemed written just for you? That is the work of the Spirit – God's personal counsel in real time, illuminating truth.

Whenever you read Scripture, ask the Holy Spirit to open your mind to understand it and to give you insight to put it into practice.

Examples of God's Counsel in Scripture

Throughout the Bible, we see how God counseled His people through His Word. To Joshua, who was facing the daunting task of leading Israel into the Promised Land, God said, *This Book of the Law shall not depart from your mouth, but you shall meditate on it day and night, so that you may be careful to do according to all that is written in it. For then you will make your way prosperous, and then you will have good success* (Joshua 1:8). Joshua was in fact prosperous – a clear indication that he obeyed all that was written in God's Word. Israel served the Lord under his leadership (Joshua 24:31), and he died with the appellation, *the servant of the Lord* (v. 29).

David, a man after God's own heart (Acts 13:22), viewed God's Word as a daily guide. In Psalm 17:4-5, he wrote, *By the word of your lips I have avoided the ways of the violent. My steps have held fast to your paths; my feet have not slipped.* God's counsel helped him stay pure and upright.

God's Word deterred the author of Psalm 119 from sinning. He insisted on meditating on it and memorizing it, saying, *I have stored up your word in my heart, that I might not sin against you* (Psalm 119:11).

Even Jesus, though fully God, modeled for us a life submitted to the counsel of Scripture. The Word was

His authority in every temptation, conflict, and teaching moment. When tempted by Satan, Jesus responded three times with *It is written* (Matthew 4:1-11), drawing from Old Testament Scripture.

God speaks to us through His Word, and when we resolve to hear His voice and obey it, we begin to see clearly His design and direction for our lives.

How God's Word Counsels Us Today

There are many ways that God instructs and counsels us in Scripture.

1. God convicts of sin through His Word.
Before we can grow, we must first be convicted. The Word exposes areas of disobedience and calls us to repentance. James likens the Bible to a mirror. When we look into it, we see ourselves as we truly are (James 1:22-25). Conviction is a form of counsel. It is God lovingly saying, "This must change." David said, *Search me, O God, and know my heart! Try me and know my thoughts!* (Psalm 139:23).

God's Word is faithful to convict us of sin. That's one of the reasons that the psalmist could rejoice, saying, *How sweet are your words to my taste, sweeter than honey to my mouth! Through your precepts I get understanding; therefore I hate every false way* (Psalm 119:103-104).

2. God gives wisdom through His Word.
The psalmist said, *Your commandment makes me wiser than my enemies, for it is ever with me. I have more*

understanding than all my teachers, for your testimonies are my meditation (Psalm 119:98-99). In Psalm 19:7, David said, *The testimony of the Lord is sure, making wise the simple.*

God's Word makes us wise. It is full of practical, life-giving wisdom for decisions, relationships, and daily living. Proverbs, for instance, offers insight on finances, integrity, friendships, speech, and more. Most importantly, Scripture makes us *wise for salvation through faith in Christ Jesus* (2 Timothy 3:15). God's Word and His Spirit lead to the knowledge of truth.

3. God renews our minds through His Word.

Romans 12:2 urges us, *Do not be conformed to this world, but be transformed by the renewal of your mind.* God uses His Word to change the way we think. Our thinking shifts from worldly patterns to kingdom patterns. With renewed minds, we no longer desire the things of the world, but we live to honor and obey God and to serve others. As Scripture renews our minds, God's ongoing, daily counsel transforms us from the inside out.

4. God comforts our hearts through His Word.

When the soul is weary, His Word brings comfort. When I (J.A.J.) am discouraged or distressed, I often turn to the book of Psalms for comfort. It is comforting to hear words such as *This I know, that God is for me* (56:9) and *He only is my rock and my salvation, my fortress; I shall not be shaken* (62:6). God speaks words of consolation and relief in Scripture, bringing joy to the heart (19:8). The promises of Scripture offer the kind of deep, sustaining encouragement that human words often cannot.

5. God directs our steps through His Word.
While not every decision in life has a direct verse attached to it, the Word of God shapes the kind of person we are becoming, which in turn influences the decisions we make. Paul commended the Thessalonian believers, saying, *The word of God* is *at work in you believers* (1 Thessalonians 2:13). The Bible is full of real and living power, at work in us to transform us and show us how to live. The psalmist said, *You guide me with your counsel* (Psalm 73:24). Solomon wrote that *the heart of man plans his ways, but the LORD establishes his steps* (Proverbs 16:9). This scriptural truth should give all believers comfort and confidence that God's guidance leads us in the right path (Psalm 23:3).

Why We Often Neglect God's Counsel

If God's counsel is so rich and accessible, why do we so often neglect it? There are many reasons (none of which are reasonable!). First, we are distracted. The noise of the world drowns out the still, small voice of God (1 Kings 19:12). Social media, news, entertainment, and even well-meaning people can dominate our attention, leaving little room for the Word.

We are also very busy. We have so many things going on in our lives that we do not devote time for the things that matter most. Many people are so busy that time alone with God is not a reality for them. There's just no time for it. There could be time if God's Word was a priority, but for many Christians, it is not.

Self-reliance also contributes to our neglect of God's counsel. Pride tells us that we can figure things out on our own. We most likely will consult Google before we consult God.

Then there's impatience. We ignore God's Word because we want immediate answers. God's counsel often requires us to wait, meditate, and seek. David said, *I waited patiently for the LORD; he inclined to me and heard my cry* (Psalm 40:1).

Finally, we are intimidated. Some people avoid Scripture because they feel they won't understand it. They have this preconceived notion that the Bible is confusing, so they avoid it altogether. While the Bible does have some difficult passages, the majority of Scripture is understandable. If we will invest the time to study it, the Holy Spirit will help us understand even the difficult parts (1 Corinthians 2:12-13).

The Power of God's Word

In a world filled with conflicting opinions and fleeting advice, God offers something eternal and trustworthy – His divine counsel. It is never out of date and never wrong. It may not always tell us what we want to hear, but it will always tell us what we need to hear.

When you allow God to be your counselor, you are choosing to receive wisdom from the Creator of the universe. There is no greater adviser or higher authority you could ever access. His wisdom outshines any self-help book. His guidance surpasses that of any professional counselor. His instruction transcends the knowledge of any scholar or seminarian.

God's counsel never falls short. In the words of Joshua to the people of Israel, *Not one word has failed of all the good things that the LORD your God promised concerning you. All have come to pass for you; not one of them has failed* (Joshua 23:14).

The chapters that follow will introduce you to an invaluable approach of Bible reading and journaling that will help you receive God's counsel in a way that daily impacts your life. Through a simple journaling approach called the GRIP method, you will learn to hear God's voice and apply what He is speaking to you.

If you've never journaled before or have done so in the past and did not like it, we are challenging you to give the GRIP method a chance. I believe it will help the Bible come alive to you in new, refreshing, and life-changing ways.

Before we look at the GRIP method, we will first discuss the importance of establishing a set time each day to spend with Jesus.

Chapter 2

Use Your Quiet Time to Journal God's Word to You

In 1845, William W. Walford penned a hymn that emphasized the importance of spending time in God's presence. The first stanza says:

> Sweet hour of prayer, sweet hour of prayer,
>   That calls me from a world of care
> And bids me at my Father's throne
>   Make all my wants and wishes known!
> In seasons of distress and grief
>   My soul has often found relief,
> And oft escaped the tempter's snare
>   By thy return, sweet hour of prayer.[2]

Many believers have a daily quiet time. A quiet time is a scheduled time to silence the noise of the world

2 Ken Bible, ed., *Sing to the Lord Hymnal* (Kansas City, MO: Lillenas Publishing Company, 1993), 632.

and to draw near to God in worship, meditation, Bible reading, and prayer. Some people also refer to this time as their devotions, or "devos" for short. This dedicated time is an appointment at the Father's throne.

Some people choose to meet with the Lord early in the morning when their mind is alert. My (J.A.J.) friend Fernando wakes up at 3:30 a.m. every day for his devotions, when it is silent and free of distractions. Others choose to spend time with God in the middle of the day. And some people prefer to have quiet time at night before bed, when they can relax and put aside the cares of the day.

The time doesn't matter. *Making* time is what matters. Find a time when your heart is quietest and most receptive, and stay committed to that time.

Finding a quiet place may be challenging, depending on your living arrangement. But if it is a priority, you will find a way. Susanna Wesley, the mother of John and Charles Wesley (the founders of Methodism), found a space to meet with the Lord even amid the chaos of a bustling home. With ten children in a small house, Susanna would sit in her kitchen and toss her apron over her head to pray. That is how she found a space of quiet. She taught her children not to disturb her when her apron covered her head.[3] Be creative and find a time and space to have a quiet time with God.

R. A. Torrey, stressing the importance of having a time to be alone with God, wrote that we must not let a single day go by without allowing God to speak to our hearts:

---

3 Eric Metaxas, *Seven Women and the Secret of Their Greatness* (Nashville: Thomas Nelson, 2015), 38.

> This is the only safe course. Any day that is allowed to pass without faithful Bible study is a day thrown open to the advent into our hearts and lives of error or of sin. . . . It is at this point many fall away. They grow careless and let a day pass, or even several days pass, without going alone with God and letting Him speak to them through His Word.[4]

Andrew Murray met with God each day and encouraged his readers to do so as well. He wrote, "Let it be your business every day, in the secrecy of the inner chamber, to meet the Holy God, and to let Him see that your heart is set on the one thing needful – that you long to live as wholly and as intensely as possible in His presence and for His service."[5] In that inner chamber, we give God our full attention. We slow down. We heed His call: *Be still, and know that I am God* (Psalm 46:10).

Even Jesus had quiet time with God. Though fully divine, He regularly removed Himself from the crowds and His disciples to commune with His Father. Mark wrote, *And rising very early in the morning, while it was still dark, he departed and went out to a desolate place, and there he prayed* (Mark 1:35). If Jesus made time to be alone with the Father, how much more do we need this daily appointment?

---

4 R. A. Torrey, *How to Succeed in the Christian Life* (New York: Fleming H. Revell Company, 1906), E-book ed., Project Gutenberg, 2017.

5 Andrew Murray, *The Inner Chamber* (Fleming H. Revell Company, 1895), 12.

Without a consistent quiet time, we remain spiritually malnourished, relying on last Sunday's sermon to feed us. But God offers fresh manna every morning (Exodus 16:4-5). His Word is living and active (Hebrews 4:12), and each new day holds fresh counsel, encouragement, conviction, and grace for the journey.

The GRIP Approach to Journaling

In the chapters to follow, you will learn how to listen and respond to God's voice through the GRIP journaling method. Each letter of the GRIP acronym represents a simple, intentional step to help you interact with God's Word and voice. Before we look at each of these steps in depth, I want to discuss the value of journaling itself.

Why Journaling Matters

Many Christian authors and pastors encourage the practice of journaling. For example:

- John Piper: "I have kept a journal off and on through the years. It helps me see what God is doing and helps me fight the fight of faith with the Word."[6]
- Dallas Willard: "Journaling can become a means of grace as we reflect deeply on our experience with God."[7]

---

6 John Piper, *When I Don't Desire God* (Wheaton, IL: Crossway, 2004), 158.

7 Dallas Willard, *The Spirit of the Disciplines* (San Francisco: Harper and Row, 1988), 156.

- Ruth Haley Barton: "Journaling is one of the most powerful spiritual disciplines for paying attention to our soul."[8]
- Chip Ingram: "Take time each day to reflect and journal what God is teaching you. You'll be amazed how it changes your perspective."[9]
- Craig Groeschel: "Write it down. You are training your brain to focus on truth."[10]

Journaling has many spiritual benefits. It invites us to wrestle with what God is teaching us and our interpretation of it. It helps us process deeply rather than passively skim through Scripture. Such a practice makes us attentive listeners and active responders.

Journaling is a way of documenting the ongoing relationship between the Counselor and the counseled – God and you. When we journal, we are not merely writing down thoughts; we are reflecting on our encounter with God.

Journaling also gives us a written record of spiritual growth that we can return to when we need to remember God's faithfulness, His corrections, His callings, and His care. David often recalled the Lord's goodness and also called the people of Israel to remember. For example, he said, *Remember the wondrous works that he has done, his miracles and the judgments he uttered* (1 Chronicles 16:12).

8 Ruth Haley Barton, *Sacred Rhythms* (Downers Grove, IL: InterVarsity Press, 2006), 121.

9 Chip Ingram, *The Real God* (Grand Rapids: Baker Books, 2016), 17.

10 Craig Groeschel, *Winning the War in Your Mind* (Grand Rapids: Zondervan, 2021), 115.

I have returned to past entries of my journals many times. These are often timely reminders of how God spoke to me during different seasons of my spiritual journey. I recently read a journal entry I had written five years ago. I could tell from my writings that I had been going through a season of discouragement. In my entry, I made an intentional decision to count my blessings and the many reasons I had to rejoice. It was encouraging to reflect on what I had written. It gave me a chance to recall how God had helped me deal with my hardships and how the Holy Spirit had led me to shift my focus off my problems and onto His goodness.

Journaling facilitates several biblical practices, including meditation, application, prayer, and confession. While we are not commanded to journal, God will use this discipline to draw us closer to Christ so we can become more like Him. Something powerful happens when we put our thoughts into writing, especially when those thoughts are written under divine influence.

Tools You Will Need

To begin using the GRIP journaling approach, you will only need three simple tools:

1. A Bible: Preferably one in a translation you understand well and are willing to engage with daily.
2. A notebook or composition book: Something dedicated for your journaling. Avoid scrap paper or loose sheets; your journal is a lasting record, not something to throw away.

3. A pen or pencil: Whichever you feel most comfortable using.

Some people prefer to keep an electronic journal, using their phone, tablet, or computer. The medium does not matter. What matters is your consistency. What matters is that you hear from God, respond in obedience, and allow Him to transform your thoughts, attitudes, and behaviors.

Making Your Quiet Time a Priority

Having a quiet time should be a priority for every believer. The truth is that we make time for what we value. In a world in which distractions are abundant, we must choose what matters most. A quiet time is not about adding something else to a busy schedule. It is about starting (or ending) your day with the one who orders your steps and renews your mind.

Set a daily time, choose a place, and guard that space. Whether it is in the early morning before the household stirs, on your lunch break, or at night before bed, find a time that works for you – and guard it. It may take effort to make it a habit, but soon it will become your most cherished time – something you look forward to every day.

God is not distant. He is near. He is a speaking God. He delights to counsel those who seek Him. Through your quiet time and GRIP journaling, you will begin to hear His voice more clearly and trust Him more deeply.

Don't worry if you've never journaled before or

if your schedule seems overwhelming. As you begin the GRIP approach, you will be amazed at the things God reveals to you. Watch and see how He guides you, counsels you, and leads you in the way everlasting.

Things to Consider as You Prepare to Begin the GRIP Method

Before you learn how to journal using GRIP, we would like to encourage you to answer two questions:

1. What time of day can I set aside to meet with God consistently? Determine a time and guard it at all costs. Effective quiet times require consistency.
2. What distractions might I need to minimize or eliminate in order to have a true quiet time? Your phone or tablet may be such a distraction, as well as potential interruptions from people. Devise a game plan for handling distractions so you can protect your quiet time.

We are now ready to walk through the GRIP journaling process. In the next chapter, we will focus on the G of GRIP.

Chapter 3

Keep a Tight GRIP on God's Word

In *Lead Like Christ,* A. W. Tozer argued that believers in Christ need a "tight grip" on the Word of God: "This does not mean knowing all of the stories in the Bible. We need to know what the Bible teaches and how it affects our lives today."[11]

To truly walk in the counsel of God, we must do more than casually handle Scripture. We must cling to it, wrestle with it, meditate on it, and allow it to grip us as we grip it. Paul urged Timothy to hold fast *the pattern of sound words* (2 Timothy 1:13), a call not merely to orthodoxy but to an anchored life.

The GRIP approach to journaling is a method that will help you listen intentionally to the living voice of God each day. Jesus said, *Man shall not live by bread alone, but by every word that comes from the mouth of*

11 A. W. Tozer, *Lead Like Christ: Reflecting the Qualities and Character of Christ in Your Ministry* (Minneapolis: Bethany House Publishers, 2021), 99.

God (Matthew 4:4). If we are going to live by the Word, we must learn how to receive it deeply.

When journaling using the GRIP approach, you structure each journal entry around four sections:

G – God's Word
R – Revelation
I – Implementation
P – Prayer

In this chapter, we will focus on G – God's Word – and how to begin journaling by centering our attention on a particular verse or passage. Following are some steps to get you started.

Step 1: Use a Bible Reading Plan

Keeping a tight grip on God's Word requires a commitment to a regular and structured reading plan. Those without a plan typically read Scripture from their favorite books, or they simply open up their Bibles and read the first page they turn to (we used to call this Bible roulette). God can obviously speak to us no matter which passage we turn to, but a Bible reading plan helps us engage *the whole counsel of God* (Acts 20:27). A reading plan presses us to read parts of the Bible we might not choose to read on our own.

Some believers follow an annual Bible reading plan that walks them through the entire Bible in a year (See Resource 3 for a 365-day reading plan). Others follow thematic or topical plans (see Resources 4 to 7 for topical plans). Still others prefer book-by-book studies, such as a focused journey through Psalms, Proverbs, or one of Paul's letters.

Choose a plan that aligns with your current season and need. Your goal is to slowly feast on God's Word and allow it to speak to your soul. Charles H. Spurgeon said, "A Bible that is falling apart usually belongs to someone who isn't."[12] A well-used Bible reflects a well-fed heart.

Step 2: Slowly Read God's Word in Your Quiet Time

Once you have selected your reading plan, approach your quiet time with reverence and expectation. Don't rush. The goal is not just comprehension – it is also communion. E. M. Bounds wrote, "Hurried devotions make weak, feeble convictions, questionable piety. To be little with God is to be little for God."[13] That is a powerful statement! Another way to say it is that to spend much time with God is to be much for God.

On a personal note, prior to 2018, I (D.N.J.) would have described my approach to reading through the Bible as "old school" – and not in a flattering way. My method amounted to sitting down for about forty-five minutes each day and willing my way through the Scriptures. On the surface, that may sound admirable. In practice, it was far less consistent than I would have liked to admit.

My problem was never desire. It was direction. I

---

12 Charles H. Spurgeon, *Morning and Evening* (Peabody, MA: Hendrickson Publishers, 2006), 23.

13 E. M. Bounds, *Power Through Prayer* (Chicago: Moody Publishing, 2009), 107.

had no clear plan, and without a plan, good intentions eventually surrender to the demands of a busy day. Some mornings I would read for an extended stretch; other days I would miss entirely. Over time, what began with genuine resolve became erratic at best. I was not failing for lack of love for God's Word; I was failing for lack of structure. That began to change in 2018 through a simple but pointed question from a pastor friend. He asked me, "What method are you using to read through the Bible each year?"

My vague answer said everything. He listened graciously, then gently challenged me. He introduced me to the Dwell Audio Bible App and encouraged me to consider it – not as a substitute for reading Scripture, but as a complement to it, a way of strengthening and sustaining my daily intake of God's Word.

I took his counsel seriously. After spending some time exploring the app, I was immediately drawn to its thoughtful design. I could select the English Standard Version (my favorite translation), choose from several voice narrations, adjust the listening speed, and even add ambient background music that aided concentration rather than pulled me away from the text. Most significantly, the app offered a structured plan for listening and reading through the entire Bible in a year – precisely what I had been lacking.

That year marked a genuine turning point in my life. I committed myself to not only listening to the assigned passages each day, but also to reading the same text afterward. This dual approach – hearing and then reading – proved remarkably effective. The apostle Paul wrote that *faith comes from hearing, and hearing through the word of Christ* (Romans 10:17). There is something powerful about engaging more than one sense when receiving Scripture. Listening allowed me to grasp the broader movement and tone of a passage. Reading then slowed me down to observe specific details, sit with a phrase, and allow truth to settle more deeply into my thinking. Together, the two disciplines reinforced one another in ways that neither accomplished alone.

Since 2018, I have not deviated from this pattern. It has become a daily anchor. Do I still occasionally miss a day? Yes. But the difference now is that I have a plan – and having a plan means that a missed day no longer derails me. I simply return to where I left off and keep moving. What once felt like an uphill struggle now feels sustainable, even natural. And over the years, I have noticed that missed days have grown increasingly rare – not simply because my discipline has improved, but because my hunger for God's Word has deepened.

What continues to astonish me is this: The Word of God never grows stale. Year after year, passage after passage, I encounter something I had not seen before. Truths I have read dozens of times before suddenly come alive with fresh clarity. Convictions deepen. Insights sharpen. Applications grow more personal and more specific. The text itself has not changed, but the Spirit of God is continuously and faithfully illuminating it. He meets the reader who returns to the Word with open hands and an expectant heart.

The writer of Hebrews declares that *the word of*

God is living and active, sharper than any two-edged sword (Hebrews 4:12). You can read the same passage a hundred times, and on the one-hundred-and-first time, the Lord will meet you there again – speaking, correcting, encouraging, and quietly transforming you from the inside out.

If there is one lesson I have learned over these years, it is this: Consistency in God's Word does not happen by accident. It is the fruit of intentional structure, a humble heart, and a settled willingness to show up every day. But when you do – when you build that rhythm and protect it – the rewards extend far beyond mere biblical knowledge. Spiritual formation deepens. Intimacy with God grows. Your ministry becomes less of something you perform and more of something that flows from an inner life genuinely shaped by Scripture.

Here are a few suggestions for attentive reading:

- Begin with prayer. Ask the Holy Spirit to open your eyes to see what He wants to show you (Psalm 119:18).
- Read aloud. Hearing the Word can sometimes help you engage differently than reading silently.
- Use a pen or highlighter. Mark verses that stand out. Underline phrases. Circle key words. Do not be afraid to mark up your Bible.
- Read with pauses. Let the Word sink in. Do not be afraid to stop and reflect as you go.

When reading attentively, some verses will seem to resonate deeply. These are the "God is speaking to me" moments. Do not rush past them. Pay attention. They may become the foundation for your journal entry.

Step 3: Review and Choose One Verse or Passage
After you read, take a moment to look back at what stood out to you. From the verses or passages that caught your attention, choose one that speaks most directly to your heart. Ask:

- What verse stirred my spirit or challenged my thinking?
- What word or phrase lingered in my mind?
- What verse speaks to a current issue or situation in my life?

The verse you select may surprise you; it may not be the obvious verse. For example, when reading John 3, the famous John 3:16 clearly stands out. But the verse that may be speaking to your heart may be something entirely different, such as John 3:30: *He must increase, but I must decrease.* Be sensitive to a verse or verses that the Holy Spirit is drawing you to.

Step 4: Write a Large "G" in Your Journal
Turn to a fresh page in your journal. (Leave the first three pages of your journal blank. You will use these pages to create a Table of Contents of your journal entries.) On the left-hand side of the page, write a large "G"; this represents God's Word.

Step 5: Write Out or Summarize the Verse(s)
Next to the G, write out the verse or passage that you selected. If it is longer (it could be several verses), summarize the main thought in one or two sentences using your own words. This not only reinforces your memory, but it also ensures that you understand the central truth. (For sample journal entries, see Resource 2.)

This part of your journal entry is the anchor. Everything else that follows – Revelation, Implementation, and Prayer – hinges on this verse (or summary of verses). Your journal entry using GRIP does not chronicle random thoughts; you will be responding to a Word from God and allowing Him to counsel you. This is life-altering reading. Donald Whitney writes, "To read the Bible is to hear God speaking. To meditate on the Bible is to prepare the heart for transformation."[14]

As you meditate on this verse or verses and begin to reflect on it, God will renew your mind (Romans 12:2), and your grip on His Word will be strengthened.

When beginning the GRIP journaling method, remember that the G in your journal is more than a letter. It is the recognition that your devotions are based on God's Word, enabling His Word to dwell richly in you (Colossians 3:16). Many believers have quiet times without Scripture being their primary focus. They may reflect upon a nice devotional reading and pray, but they are not diving deeply into the Word of God. Their daily experience with God is not rooted and grounded in scriptural truth.

---

14 Donald Whitney, *Spiritual Disciplines for the Christian Life* (Colorado Springs: NavPress, 1991), 47.

John Piper notes that "we must seek to understand the Bible's meaning, and we must pause to contemplate what we understand, and, by the Spirit, to feel and express the appropriate response of the heart."[15]

When you build your life on Scripture – verse by verse, one encounter at a time – you begin to think, feel, and live differently. You begin to walk in the counsel of God. You begin to grip the Word, and more importantly, you begin to let the Word grip you.

Your Turn

Let's practice writing the G section of GRIP.

Slowly and carefully read Philippians chapters 1 and 2. As you read, be sensitive to what the Holy Spirit is speaking to you. Then reflect on the questions we looked at earlier in Step 3. Select a verse or verses that especially spoke to your heart, and write the verse (or a summary of the verses) in a journal. Don't forget to write a large "G" on the left side of the page. (If you do not have a journal yet, a starter journal is provided for you in Resource 8.)

Once you write out the verse(s) from Philippians 1 or 2, G is complete.

In the next chapter, you will learn how to write the R section of GRIP – Revelation. This is where you will discover what God is showing you in His Word.

15 John Piper, "Reading the Bible in Prayer and Communion with God," in the ESV Study Bible (Wheaton: Crossway, 2008), 2571.

Chapter 4

Record What God Reveals to You

The Bible is God speaking. Some Christians say, "God never speaks to me." However, if we consistently read and meditate on His Word, He will reveal His purpose, plans, desires, will, etc. for our lives. As Mark Driscoll and Gerry Breshears said, "The Bible is a living book of God authoritatively speaking as a perfect Father to children he dearly loves. The Bible tells us how to live godly lives."[16]

In chapter 3, we explored the first part of the GRIP method: G for God's Word. We discussed the importance of starting your journaling time with Scripture and grounding your quiet time in God's revealed truth. Now we move to the second letter – R, which stands for Revelation. Tozer understood something that is easy to miss – that the goal of Scripture is not *information*

16 Mark Driscoll and Gerry Breshears, *Doctrine: What Christians Should Believe* (Wheaton: Crossway, 2010), 67.

about God, but *communion* with Him. Revelation, at its heart, is relational. God does not simply hand us a document to quote, but He opens a window into Himself, inviting us to know Him the way a child knows a father, or a friend knows a friend – deeply, personally, and with growing delight.

A. W. Tozer wrote, "The Bible is not an end in itself, but a means to bring men to an intimate and satisfying knowledge of God, that they may enter into Him, that they may delight in His Presence."[17] Revelation is about getting to know God.

In this chapter, we will learn how to listen attentively to God's voice and capture what He reveals to us through His Spirit and Word.

God's Revelation: Personal and Present

When God reveals Himself to us in Scripture, it is personal and direct. For example, we see this principle at work in 1 Samuel 3:21: *The Lord revealed himself to Samuel at Shiloh by the word of the Lord.* Commenting on this verse, John Piper said, "The Lord *himself* is revealed by his *word*, that is, by what he *says* to us, whether audibly or in written form."[18]

This means that every time you open your Bible with a heart to hear from God, you are not merely reading ancient literature, but you are being met by a Person. The words on the page are the vehicle, but the

17 A. W. Tozer, *The Pursuit of God* (Harrisburg, PA: Christian Publications, 1948), 8.

18 John Piper, "Reading the Bible in Prayer and Communion with God," in the ESV Study Bible (Wheaton: Crossway, 2008), 2571.

destination is God Himself, who makes Himself known through them with the same directness and intimacy He showed young Samuel in the stillness of Shiloh.

God's words were personal in Samuel's case, and the same is true for us today. When we approach Scripture with a receptive heart, God reveals Himself – not just facts about Him, but His very presence, character, and intentions. "From Genesis to Revelation, God's words and God's deeds reveal God himself for our knowledge and our enjoyment."[19]

The verses and passages in your Bible aren't just words on a page. "What we discover is that it is through the words of Scripture that the living God reveals himself to us. In these writings God acts upon us."[20] When we encounter God through His Word, He is not passive. He is actively working – chiseling away the areas of our lives that do not look like Christ, renewing the minds that once conformed to the world, and stirring within us desires and convictions that we could never manufacture on our own. As Paul reminded us in Philippians 2:13, it is God Himself who is at work in us *both to will and to work for his good pleasure* – meaning that even our wanting to change is a gift He produces in us through the living power of His Word.

Journaling What God Reveals to You

Below are the steps to writing down what God reveals

19 Piper, "Reading the Bible," 2571.

20 Kelly M. Kapic, *A Little Book for New Theologians* (Downers Grove, IL: IVP Academic, 2012), 106.

to you in His Word. The GRIP method helps you organize and capture these insights so you can return to them, meditate on them, and live them out.

Step 1: Write a Large "R" in Your Journal

After you've completed the G (God's Word) portion of your journal entry, leave a space underneath and write a large "R." This signifies your transition from reading Scripture to describing what God is revealing to you.

Step 2: Determine What God Is Revealing to You

This is the heart of the journaling process. Ask the Holy Spirit to open your eyes and your understanding. The Holy Spirit reveals God's wisdom and searches the deep things of God (1 Corinthians 2:10). He allows us to understand what God has freely given us (v. 12).

As you ponder the passage you have read, ask questions like these:

1. What has God revealed to me about Himself?

   What name, character trait, or attribute of God is evident in this passage? Is He revealing His love, justice, mercy, sovereignty, holiness, or faithfulness?

2. What has God revealed to me about His purposes?

   What do you see about God's will and His plans – either for humanity in general or for you specifically? Is He showing you what He wants to accomplish in your life, family, church, or circumstances?

3. What has God revealed to me about His ways?

   God has specific ways of working. He often uses suffering to shape character, grace to break pride, and delays to strengthen trust. What patterns of divine behavior are present in the passage? How does God act? How does He respond?

4. What has God revealed to me about Jesus?

   Jesus is the radiance of God's glory and the exact imprint of His nature (Hebrews 1:3). Ask: What does this passage show me about Christ – His person, His work, His grace, His heart, His invitation to me? How does this passage point to the gospel?

5. What has God revealed to me about myself?

   Scripture is a mirror (James 1:23-25). What does it show about your character, thoughts, emotions, behaviors, or needs? Is God revealing an area in which you need healing, correction, or growth?

When you ask what God is revealing, remember that He reveals truth not for trivia's sake, but to transform you into Christlikeness. Revelation is an invitation to respond.

Step 3: Write Down What God Reveals to You

Once you have prayerfully identified what God is revealing, write it down under the R in your journal. Be specific. Don't just write what sounds spiritual, but write what God is speaking to you through the verse or verses you wrote down in the G section of your journal entry. The things you write may be uncomfortable, especially if God is correcting you. Exercise humility as you write down what God reveals.

Sometimes your writing may be a paragraph or two describing how God spoke to your heart. Other times it might be a sentence or even a single phrase. Do not be concerned about the length. Rather, focus on what God is saying to you.

There are many benefits to putting your words in writing. It reinforces learning. It clarifies your thoughts. It also creates a permanent record of God's faithfulness in your life, allowing you to come back months later, or even years later, and trace God's hand at work in your spiritual journey.

Examples of Revelation

For the first example below, the Scripture I (J.A.J.) read during my quiet time was Jeremiah 32. For R, I answered the question: What does God reveal about Himself?

Example 1
G – *Behold, I am the Lord, the God of all flesh. Is anything too hard for me?* (Jeremiah 32:27).

R – In Jeremiah 32, God reveals Himself as an all-powerful God who has power to accomplish His purposes. Nothing is too difficult for Him. He created the universe and is sovereign over all creation. Absolutely nothing is too hard for my God, and I must never doubt His power. He can make a way where there seems to be no way.

Example 2
In this next example, I answered the question, What has God revealed to me about His purposes?

G – *I have been crucified with Christ. It is no longer I who live, but Christ who lives in me. And the life I now live in the flesh I live by faith in the Son of God* (Galatians 2:20).

R – This verse reveals God's purpose for me: to live a life of surrender – one that reflects Christ's presence and power within me. Paul was so surrendered to Christ that he lived his life as if Christ was actually living out His life through him. He said, *It is no longer I who live.* Wow!

Example 3
This example is based on 1 Timothy 6. For R, I answered the question, What has God revealed to me about myself?

G – *Godliness with contentment is great gain. . . . If we have food and clothing, with these we will be content* (1 Timothy 6:6, 8).

R – I am never satisfied. I always want more. Enough is never enough. God is teaching me to be content with what I have. I have more than adequate clothing, and I eat quite well. God has given me everything I need. I do not lack anything. I am ungrateful, and this needs to change.

Example 4
In this final example, I read 2 Timothy 4 during my quiet time. For R, I again answered the question, What has God revealed to me about myself?

G – *For Demas, in love with this present world, has deserted me and gone to Thessalonica* (2 Timothy 4:10).

R – Paul gives a biography of Demas in six words: *in love with this present world.* Demas's love for the world prevented him from serving God. This is an ongoing struggle I have as well. I love this present world too much. I want all the things this world has to offer, including materialistic things, pleasure, and entertainment. And these things prevent me from being all in with God.

The Value of Revelation

God desires to reveal Himself. Jesus said, *He who loves me will be loved by my Father, and I will love him and manifest myself to him* (John 14:21). The more you listen for God's voice, the more He will reveal areas of your life that are not conformed to Christ.

Take "R" seriously. Recording what God reveals is a way to say, "Lord, I am listening. I treasure Your words more than anything else." Do not be in a rush when you are discerning what the Lord is speaking to you. E. M. Bounds said, "It takes good time for the full flow of God into the spirit. Short devotions can cut the pipe of God's flow. It takes time in the secret places to get full revelation of God."[21]

Your Turn

Let's continue to practice journaling. In the last chapter, you wrote down a verse or a summary of verses from Philippians 1 or 2 for the G section of your journal entry. Now write a large "R" and record what God spoke to your heart. Be sure to revisit the questions in Step 2. They will help you discern what the Holy Spirit wants to teach you.

In the next chapter, we will explore the "I" in GRIP – Implementation – and how to apply what God has revealed to your daily life. When revelation is followed by obedient action, real life change takes place.

21 E. M. Bounds, *Power Through Prayer* (Chicago: Moody Publishing, 2009), 107.

Chapter 5

Implement God's Word

Although Scripture was written long ago in lands far away, its message is not confined to ancient cultures or outdated settings. Scripture speaks directly to us, here and now.

Deuteronomy 29:29 reminds us that *the things that are revealed belong to us and to our children forever, that we may do all the words of this law.* Paul echoed this truth: *For whatever was written in former days was written for our instruction, that through endurance and through the encouragement of the Scriptures we might have hope* (Romans 15:4). He also said in 1 Corinthians 10:11, *Now these things happened to them as an example, but they were written down for our instruction.*

The Bible is *living and active* (Hebrews 4:12) and relevant for today. That is why Paul could declare, *All Scripture is breathed out by God and profitable for teaching, for reproof, for correction, and for training in righteousness, that the man of God may be complete, equipped for every good work* (2 Timothy 3:16-17).

Reading God's Word for Life Transformation

The very same Word that God spoke in ancient times is the same Word that transforms lives today. God's Word is alive. There is a barrier, however, that prevents many believers from allowing the Bible to take root in their hearts and bear fruit in their lives. This barrier arises when they approach Scripture academically – without the expectation that it can produce an immediate or practical result. When Scripture reading is an academic exercise, people read merely for information or knowledge. Knowledge is good, of course, but if biblical instruction is not lived out in their lives – shaping their attitudes and behaviors – all that knowledge is simply worthless.

God's Word is an invitation to transformation, empowering us to become conformed to the image of Christ (Romans 8:29). James writes, *But be doers of the word, and not hearers only, deceiving yourselves* (James 1:22). He says that the one who hears but fails to apply it is like someone who looks in a mirror and then forgets what he looks like. In contrast, *the one who looks into the perfect law, the law of liberty, and perseveres, . . . will be blessed in his doing* (James 1:25).

Jesus Himself taught this principle in John 13:17: *If you know these things, blessed are you if you do them.* He also said, *Everyone who hears these words of mine and does not do them will be like a foolish man who built his house on the sand. And the rain fell, and the floods came, and the winds blew and beat against that house, and it fell, and great was the fall of it* (Matthew 7:26-27).

Knowledge of God's Word is not the end goal;

obedience is. The blessing is not in the hearing alone, but in the doing of God's Word. J. C. Ryle wrote, "What we apply to ourselves is the part that does us good. The rest may feed the intellect, but does not sanctify the heart."[22] He understood the same truth that every growing Christian must embrace: Scripture must be acted upon.

Implementing What God Reveals: The I in GRIP

In your GRIP journal, you have already read God's Word (G) and sought to discern what He is revealing to you (R). Now comes the crucial next step: Implementation – determining how you will obey what God has revealed.

Step 1: Write a Large "I" in Your Journal

After you've completed the R (Revelation) section of your journal entry, skip a space and write a large "I," which stands for Implementation. This marks your transition from hearing to doing.

Step 2: Determine What God Wants You to Implement into Your Life

As you consider what God is calling you to do, ask Him for guidance. George Mueller, a man of extraordinary faith and prayer, developed a powerful set of questions to help him apply Scripture personally:

- Is there an example for me to follow?

22 J. C. Ryle, *Practical Religion* (Edinburgh: Banner of Truth Trust, 2015), 144.

- Is there a command for me to obey?
- Is there an error for me to avoid?
- Is there a sin for me to forsake?
- Is there a promise for me to claim?
- Is there any new thought about God Himself?[23]

These six questions will sharpen your spiritual sensitivity. Ask them prayerfully. Then listen. What is God pointing out? What adjustments is He inviting you to make? What acts of obedience do you know God wants you to take? What scriptural truth does He want you to implement into your life?

Robert Boyd reminds us to "submit unhesitatingly" to all of the Bible's teachings. He writes, "Study and accept not only what you like, but all that God has to say (John 7:17)."[24]

Step 3: Write Down What You Will Implement into Your Life

Now record the specific action or response God is calling you to make. Do not settle for vague intentions like "I need to trust God more." Instead, be clear and practical. For example, "This week I will surrender my anxiety about money to God by refusing to complain, and instead I will pray Philippians 4:6-7 every morning." This gives your implementation shape and direction.

23 George Mueller, *Quiet Time: An InterVarsity Guidebook for Daily Devotions*, Revised Edition (Downers Grove, IL: InterVarsity Press, 1976), 21.

24 Robert Boyd, *First Words to New Christians* (Abbotsford, WI: Aneko Press, 2020), eBook. The quote comes from Appendix A: How to Use the Bible.

Examples of G – R – I

In the previous chapter, we provided several examples of how to journal G and R. Here are the same examples along with the Implementation section of GRIP.

Example 1
G – *Behold, I am the Lord, the God of all flesh. Is anything too hard for me?* (Jeremiah 32:27).

R – In Jeremiah 32, God reveals Himself as an all-powerful God who has power to accomplish His purposes. Nothing is too difficult for Him. He created the universe and is sovereign over all creation. Absolutely nothing is too hard for my God, and I must never doubt His power. He can make a way where there seems to be no way.

I – The strain between my daughter and me is unbearable. It doesn't even seem like she cares about me or wants to reconcile with me. If nothing is too hard for God, surely He can and will intervene in my situation. He has sovereignty over all flesh and is able to restore my broken relationship. I put my faith and trust in God right now to bring healing.

Example 2
G – *I have been crucified with Christ. It is no longer I who live, but Christ who lives in me. And the life I now live in the flesh I live by faith in the Son of God* (Galatians 2:20).

R – This verse reveals God's purpose for me: to live a life of surrender – one that reflects Christ's presence and power within me. Paul was so surrendered to Christ that he lived his life as if Christ was actually living out His life through him. He said, *It is no longer I who live.* Wow!

I – God is reminding me that my old life is dead. Jesus is in me, and I must choose to deny myself and live as if Christ is living His life through me. If it is true that Christ is living in me, I must live like it! The words I speak today – I must ask, are these the words Christ would speak? My attitudes and thoughts – is this the way Christ would think? The decisions I make – is this a decision Christ would make? The way I treat others – is this how Christ would approach others? Today, by faith in Christ, I will intentionally live as if Jesus was living His life through me.

Example 3

G – *Godliness with contentment is great gain. . . . If we have food and clothing, with these we will be content* (1 Timothy 6:6, 8).

R – I am never satisfied. I always want more. Enough is never enough. God is teaching me to be content with what I have. I have more than adequate clothing, and I eat quite well. God has given me everything I need. I do not lack anything. I am ungrateful, and this needs to change.

I – Today, I will write down five things I am thankful for, and I will share that list with a friend. This week, every time I catch myself complaining about what I don't have, I will immediately pray, "Thank You, Lord, for providing all my needs."

Example 4
G – *For Demas, in love with this present world, has deserted me and gone to Thessalonica* (2 Timothy 4:10).

R – Paul gives a biography of Demas in six words: *in love with this present world.* Demas's love for the world prevented him from serving God. This is an ongoing struggle I have as well. I love this present world too much. I want all the things this world has to offer, including materialistic things, pleasure, and entertainment. And these things prevent me from being all in with God.

I – I will fast from social media and entertainment for the next three days and will use that time to read my Bible and pray about where my affections lie. I will also memorize 1 John 2:15 this week: *Do not love the world or the things in the world.* I will make sure that I am not in love with this present world.

The Transforming Power of Application

Implementation is the turning point when God's Word moves from knowledge to transformation. Each day that you implement what God reveals, you become more and more Christlike. Each obedient step draws you nearer to the heart of God and shapes you to think, speak, and act like Jesus.

The Puritan pastor Thomas Watson said, "The reason we come away so cold from reading the word is because we do not warm ourselves at the fire of meditation."[25] We might add that the reason we come away unchanged is because we fail to obey. The Word of God is a fire and a hammer (Jeremiah 23:29), and when it is implemented, it reshapes our minds, breaks stubborn habits, heals wounded hearts, and renews our lives.

God is ready to counsel you. Will you dedicate time each and every day to implement what He reveals?

Your Turn

Let's continue to practice GRIP. In chapter three, you selected a verse or summary of verses from Philippians 1 and 2. In chapter four, you described what God revealed to you from this verse or verses. Now it is time to determine how you will apply this passage to your life.

Turn to your journal and write a big "I." If you know what God is asking you to apply to your life, write it down. If you are unsure, review the six questions under Step 2 to help you.

In the next chapter, we will look at "P" and discuss how to conclude our journal entries with heartfelt prayers.

---

25 Thomas Watson, *Heaven Taken by Storm* (Morgan, PA: Soli Deo Gloria Publications, 1992), 65.

Chapter 6

Commune with God Through Prayer

When we begin our quiet time and use the GRIP approach for journaling, we begin by opening the Word of God. We conclude our devotions by opening our hearts to God through prayer. The fourth part of the GRIP approach, P – Prayer, allows us to commune with the Lord in a personal and scripturally guided way.

Prayer is our response to all that God has shown us. It is not just an afterthought to reading Scripture, but is the culmination of divine communication. God has spoken through His Word and Spirit, and now we respond. This relational, Spirit-led exchange becomes the lifeblood of spiritual growth and inner transformation.

The Bible constantly invites us to pray (e.g., Philippians 4:6; 1 Thessalonians 5:17), and we are shown in the life of Christ that prayer is essential to intimacy with God. Jesus demonstrated such closeness in John 17 when He prayed for Himself (vv. 1-5), His disciples (vv. 6-19), and for future believers (vv. 20-26). He especially exhibited intimacy with His Father in the garden of Gethsemane (Matthew 26:36-46) when He expressed the overwhelming distress He was about to face.

Prayer not only cultivates intimacy with God, but it is also the key to spiritual victory. Jesus said, *And whatever you ask in prayer, you will receive, if you have faith* (Matthew 21:22). Charles Spurgeon was well aware that God's power is unleashed through prayer. He wrote, "Prayer is the slender nerve that moves the muscle of omnipotence."[26]

In this chapter, you will learn how to write the final part of your GRIP journal entry – the "P." You will learn to craft a prayer that flows from what God has spoken to your heart. At the end of the chapter, we will discuss how to organize your journal with titles and a Table of Contents so you can revisit the ways God has counseled you over time.

The Power and Importance of Prayer

Prayer is where the truths of Scripture become personal. Through prayer, we:

- Thank God for His Word and His ways.
- Confess where we fall short.
- Praise Him for who He is.

26 Charles H. Spurgeon, *The Power in Prayer* (New Kensington, PA: Whitaker House, 1993), 19.

- Ask for strength to obey.
- Intercede for others and ourselves.

This is how we draw near to our Counselor, Father, and Friend. We commune with God through words that arise from a heart that has been convicted and surrendered. Your prayers do not need to be polished or eloquent. They just need to be real. Dwight L. Moody wrote, "It is not the most beautiful or eloquent language that brings the answer; it is the cry that goes up from a burdened heart."[27] God has never been impressed by polished prayers. He is moved by honest ones, and there is no heart so burdened that He will not hear it.

Journaling Your Prayer

Here are the steps to write this final piece of your GRIP journal entry.

Step 1: Write a Large "P" in Your Journal
After completing the I (Implementation) section, move to the next space in your journal and write a large "P."

Step 2: Write Your Prayer as a Personal Response to God
In this step, you are not just writing a random prayer. You are writing a personal response to something specific that God revealed to your heart. Do not let this be a generic prayer. It should be heartfelt and guided

27 Dwight L. Moody, *Prevailing Prayer: A Thorough Study on the Subject of Prayer* (Abbotsford, WI: Aneko Press, 2018), 108-109.

by the Spirit. It should also be faith-filled. Remember, Jesus said that you will receive whatever you ask in prayer *if you have faith* (Matthew 21:22).

Here are a few types of prayers you might write, depending on what the Lord has revealed:

Confession: "Lord, forgive me for harboring bitterness against my mother-in-law. You've shown me that I cannot carry this any longer. Cleanse my heart and give me Your peace."

Thanksgiving: "Thank You for reminding me that You are my provider. I trust that You will help me find a job. I am thanking You in advance for coming through for me and my family!"

Praise: "You are my Rock and my Redeemer! I worship You because You never change, and because Your Word is always true. You are a great and mighty God, and I give You glory and praise!"

Petition: "Help me guard my mouth today as I speak to my wife. I need Your Spirit to control my tongue so that I speak kindness, not anger. Please guide my words."

Intercession: "Lord, I am believing You to work in my child's heart. Draw him back to You. Surround him with godly influences. Place people in his life that will point him to You. You said that if I ask anything in Your name, it will be done. I am asking in the name of Jesus and believing!"

Keep in mind that your prayer may be a combination of different types of prayer. For example, you might begin with confession, move to intercession, and then end with thanksgiving. There is no right or wrong style of prayer. Just be sure your prayer is genuine and from the heart – not just words you are writing down to complete your entry. D. L. Moody wrote, "Very often when we cry to God, we really do not mean anything."[28] Your prayer should reflect your honest thoughts and should be shaped by the Holy Spirit's conviction and direction.

Step 3: Title Your Journal Entry

After completing the G, R, I, and P sections, write a title for your journal entry at the top of the page. The title should reflect the theme of what God spoke to you or how you responded.

Here are some examples of titles:

- "The Lord Is My Protector"
- "Guarding My Words"
- "Trusting God with My Finances"
- "The God of Miracles"
- "Letting Go of Fear"

Step 4: Add the Entry to Your Table of Contents

Your journal should begin with a few pages designated as a Table of Contents. After completing a journal entry, add the following information to the Table: title, date, Scripture passage used, and journal page number.

---

28 Moody, *Prevailing Prayer*, 108-109.

This allows you to quickly reference past entries, track your spiritual growth, and even use your entries for teaching or ministry purposes. Your journal becomes a resource – a treasure chest – of divine counsel.

Examples of GRIP

Let's revisit the examples from chapter 5 and complete them with the P section and a title for the entry.

Example 1: God of the Impossible
G – *Behold, I am the LORD, the God of all flesh. Is anything too hard for me?* (Jeremiah 32:27).

R – In Jeremiah 32, God reveals Himself as an all-powerful God who has power to accomplish His purposes. Nothing is too difficult for Him. He created the universe and is sovereign over all creation. Absolutely nothing is too hard for my God, and I must never doubt His power. He can make a way where there seems to be no way.

I – The strain between my daughter and me is unbearable. It doesn't even seem like she cares about me or wants to reconcile with me. If nothing is too hard for God, surely He can and will intervene in my situation. He has sovereignty over all flesh and is able to restore my broken relationship. I put my faith and trust in God right now to bring healing.

P – Lord, You are the God of miracles. There is nothing

that is impossible for You. Will You please intervene in my situation? Show me what I need to do or say to make things right with my daughter. Soften her heart. Please break through, in Jesus's name, I pray. Nothing is too hard for You. Thank You for bringing healing to our relationship.

Example 2: Christ in Me
G – *I have been crucified with Christ. It is no longer I who live, but Christ who lives in me. And the life I now live in the flesh I live by faith in the Son of God* (Galatians 2:20).

R – This verse reveals God's purpose for me: to live a life of surrender – one that reflects Christ's presence and power within me. Paul was so surrendered to Christ that he lived his life as if Christ was actually living out His life through him. He said, *It is no longer I who live.* Wow!

I – God is reminding me that my old life is dead. Jesus is in me, and I must choose to deny myself and live as if Christ is living His life through me. If it is true that Christ is living in me, I must live like it! The words I speak today – I must ask, are these the words Christ would speak? My attitudes and thoughts – is this the way Christ would think? The decisions I make – is this a decision Christ would make? The way I treat others – is this how Christ would approach others? Today, by faith in Christ, I will intentionally live as if Jesus was living His life through me.

P – Jesus, please continue to work in my life so that it is evident to the world that it is You living in me. May my words be Christlike. May my thoughts be Christlike. May the decisions I make and the things I do reflect Christlikeness. I pray that Galatians 2:20 will be said of me.

Example 3: Content in Christ

G – *Godliness with contentment is great gain. . . . If we have food and clothing, with these we will be content* (1 Timothy 6:6, 8).

R – I am never satisfied. I always want more. Enough is never enough. God is teaching me to be content with what I have. I have more than adequate clothing, and I eat quite well. God has given me everything I need. I do not lack anything. I am ungrateful, and this needs to change.

I – Today, I will write down five things I am thankful for and I will share that list with a friend. This week, every time I catch myself complaining about what I don't have, I will immediately pray, "Thank You, Lord, for providing all my needs."

P – Thank You for showing me that I need to find my contentment in You. You have never failed me. You prove over and over to be a good God. Please forgive me for never being satisfied. You are all I need, and I surrender any discontentment I have to You.

Example 4: Forsaking this World
G – *For Demas, in love with this present world, has deserted me and gone to Thessalonica* (2 Timothy 4:10).

R – Paul gives a biography of Demas in six words: *in love with this present world.* Demas's love for the world prevented him from serving God. This is an ongoing struggle I have as well. I love this present world too much. I want all the things this world has to offer, including materialistic things, pleasure, and entertainment. And these things prevent me from being all in with God.

I – I will fast from social media and entertainment for the next three days and will use that time to read my Bible and pray about where my affections lie. I will also memorize 1 John 2:15 this week: *Do not love the world or the things in the world.* I will make sure I am not in love with this present world.

P – Lord, please forgive me for making much of this world. I have not been living as a citizen of heaven. I've been caught up enjoying this life. I resolve today to make Christ my treasure. You are my life and my all!

For more examples of GRIP, see Resource 2: Sample Journal Entries.

We have concluded our discussion on how to journal using GRIP. The GRIP method equips us to be truly counseled by God. We rely on Him to guide and direct us, knowing that His Word has more wisdom than any counsel we can receive from man. If you commit to this journaling method, then over time, your journal will become a record of His counsel, a testimony of His faithfulness, and an archive of answered prayers.

Your Turn

Let's complete the journal entry we first began in chapter three. In your journal, write a large "P." Revisit what you wrote in your entry, and then write a prayer of response. Whether you are giving God praise, confessing a sin, or asking Him for help, be specific and be real. God longs to hear you pray.

In the next three chapters, we will discuss the ministry applications of GRIP. You will learn how to use GRIP as a tool to disciple others, prepare sermons, and counsel others.

Part 2

Ministry Applications of GRIP

Chapter 7

A Discipleship and Mentoring Tool

In Part 1 of this book, you learned how to hear God speak through the GRIP method of journaling: God's Word, Revelation, Implementation, and Prayer. We discussed how this devotional tool allows us to be counseled by God so that He can lead us, guide us, and direct all our steps. It is an approach that helps us experience life transformation as we *grow in the grace and knowledge of our Lord and Savior Jesus Christ* (2 Peter 3:18).

But this transformation is not meant to be kept to ourselves. As disciples of Christ, we are commissioned to make disciples: *Go therefore and make disciples of all nations, . . . teaching them to observe all that I have commanded* (Matthew 28:19-20). That is why in Part 2 we shift the focus from personal transformation to ministry applications. We will first examine how GRIP allows us to disciple others. Then we will discover how GRIP can assist us in sermon preparation and give us spiritual readiness to counsel others.

GRIP Groups: A Framework for Discipleship

GRIP is a powerful discipleship and mentoring tool. There are many useful discipleship resources in print, but GRIP is advantageous because one just needs a Bible, a pen, and a journal.

Throughout my (J.A.J.) ministry, I have met with other men to read God's Word and to journal together. Group journaling works well with both new believers and mature believers. I have even met weekly with my church's leadership team to dive into God's Word and journal through Scripture.

Here are the key things you need to know when using GRIP to disciple others:

Size: GRIP Groups are small gatherings of three to five individuals who meet weekly. These groups are intimate and interactive, focused on building relationships with God and each other.

Location: GRIP Groups can meet anywhere – at a leader's home, a coffee shop, a church classroom, a prison dayroom, or even outdoors. The setting should be informal and conducive to prayerful reflection and open conversation.

Reading Scripture: The group selects a chapter or two from the Bible, preferably from a systematic reading plan (see Resources 3 to 7 for several different types of reading plans). Everyone reads silently, taking in God's Word without rushing. The goal is not speed, but spiritual attentiveness.

Journaling: After reading, each person then journals through the four components of GRIP as described in Part 1.

Sharing Journal Entries: After everyone has completed the journaling process, each person shares their journal entry one by one. This is not a Bible-study discussion, but it is a time for testimony, accountability, and encouragement. As people share what God revealed, how they plan to obey, and the prayers they wrote, group members learn from each other. You will find that mutual edification is a regular part of a GRIP Group.

Equipping Opportunities: As you lead and facilitate the group, gently guide participants to rightly discern what God may be revealing. You might ask, "Is this truth consistent with what Scripture teaches elsewhere?" or "How will you practically carry this out?" As you disciple participants, your goal should be to help them grow in biblical interpretation and life application.

Encouraging Daily GRIP: Challenge the group to use GRIP journaling on their own throughout the week, not just during the group. In this way, they develop a personal habit of feeding on God's Word. Check in with them and ask them to share what God is revealing to them during their quiet times. Finally, encourage them to continue journaling if they have slacked off.

The goal of a GRIP Group is spiritual growth – to help those you are discipling to experience *mature manhood, to the measure of the stature of the fullness of Christ* (Ephesians 4:13). Your aim is to help them *grow up in every way into him who is the head, into Christ* (v. 15).

Notice Paul's words *into Christ.* Spiritual growth is a thoroughly Christ-centered thing: "It's growth into closer relationship with him, and deeper understanding of who he is and how he thinks and what he desires and what will honour him. It's growth into greater Christlikeness."[29] As you meet in GRIP groups to disciple others, you will see God at work in their lives to shape them to become more like Jesus as they learn to obey Him fully.

One-on-One Mentoring with GRIP

GRIP journaling also lends itself to one-on-one mentoring. Jesus ministered to the multitudes, but He also poured deeply into individuals – in particular, Peter, James, and John.

Mentoring is about walking alongside someone in their spiritual journey. It is personal, intentional, and relational. Whether you are meeting with a younger believer, a new convert, or someone needing encouragement, the GRIP method provides a structure for spiritual conversation.

29 Andrew M. Randall, *Following Jesus: The Essentials of Christian Discipleship* (Edinburgh: Banner of Truth Trust, 2018), 98.

When I was a young staff pastor, the senior pastor of our church modeled this to his staff. He had weekly one-on-one meetings with certain men he was mentoring, but each meeting was structured around a passage of Scripture. They read their Bibles, and then they both wrote down what God was speaking through His Word. All conversations stemmed from the Word of God. Scripture was the focus of the mentoring relationship. The men he mentored became rooted and grounded in God's Word, and many of them became leaders themselves.

GRIP provides a framework for this type of life-changing mentoring. Here is how GRIP can be used in a mentoring context:

1. Ask your mentee to journal through a specific Bible passage using GRIP before your meeting.
2. When you meet, both you and your mentee share your journal entries.
3. You, as the mentor, should model depth of reflection and transparency. Be sure your journal entries are authentic. Don't write to impress or to show how spiritual you are. Be real and write what God is revealing to you about your life and your struggles. Jim Putnam and Bobby Harrington said, "The biblical model for church community is an authentic and healthy transparency that repeatedly points people back to the gospel. It is never healthy to try covering sin or hiding it away."[30]

30 Jim Putnam and Bobby Harrington, *DiscipleShift: Five Steps That Help Your Church to Make Disciples Who Make Disciples* (Grand Rapids: Zondervan, 2013), 104.

The more transparent you are about your own struggles, the more your mentees will open up about their struggles and battles, which will allow you to speak gospel truth into their lives. Also, be receptive to any insights they have about your life.

As you and your mentee share what God revealed through GRIP, then spiritual growth, accountability, and personal connection are cultivated. Your goal is not to teach a lesson. Instead, GRIP becomes the shared curriculum, and the Holy Spirit becomes the teacher.

Teaching GRIP to Those You Lead

GRIP has additional discipleship applications. Leaders of all kinds – pastors, Bible study leaders, youth pastors, chaplains, men's and women's ministry leaders, etc. – can equip others to hear God's voice through GRIP. Too often, churchgoers rely solely on Sunday sermons for spiritual nourishment. But one meal a week is not enough. Job valued God's Word more than provision for his own physical well-being. He said, *I have not departed from the commandments of his lips; I have treasured the words of his mouth more than my portion of food* (Job 23:12).

We must teach believers how to feed themselves daily from God's Word. GRIP is a practical, replicable method for spiritual self-feeding. Here are a few ways to implement GRIP in your leadership:

- Church Discipleship Tracks: Incorporate GRIP into new-believer classes or discipleship programs.

- Youth and College Ministry: Teach GRIP to young believers to build lifelong habits of listening to God.
- Chaplaincy and Recovery Programs: GRIP is especially helpful in settings where structure, accountability, and personal reflection are vital.
- Church Plants: Church planters can use GRIP as a discipleship and mentoring tool during all phases of church planting (e.g., discipling members of the launch team, discipling new believers, and mentoring potential leaders).

The job of the spiritual leader is not to create spiritual dependence, but spiritual maturity. GRIP trains believers to engage with the living Word of God on their own. Faithful discipleship always depends upon the Scriptures as the avenue of God's voice for His people.

GRIP for Parents and Families

Parents are the primary disciplers of their children. The Bible instructs us to teach God's Word diligently to our kids – when we sit in our house, when we walk by the way, when we lie down, and when we rise (Deuteronomy 6:6-7).

GRIP is a tool that families can use together, helping children learn how to hear God's voice from a young age. When using GRIP during family devotions, choose a short passage. Let each family member write or draw something in a GRIP journal. If you need to make age-appropriate adaptations, then help children identify what stood out (G), what it means (R), how to obey (I), and encourage them to write or say a simple prayer (P). Then take turns sharing what everyone wrote.

It is valuable to teach your children Bible stories, but you will teach them how to be counseled by God by showing them how to interact with God personally through His living and active Word. It is also important to model by example. Putman and Harrington observed, "Modeling plays such a huge part in parenting and disciple making."[31]

Let your children see you studying God's Word in your own time. Let them see you writing what God reveals to you. Let them see you praying. That is the greatest legacy we can leave as parents.

The GRIP method has many applications for discipleship. As you lead GRIP Groups, mentor individuals, train your congregation, or teach your children, you are helping others learn to hear from God, obey Him, and walk with Him daily.

We are not meant to merely consume God's Word; we are commanded to pass it on, teaching others to obey all that Christ has commanded (Matthew 28:19-20). GRIP gives you an organized way to do so.

In the next chapter, we will see how the GRIP method gives us a lasting spiritual record and an endless supply of Spirit-inspired sermons and teachings.

31 Putnam and Harrington, *DiscipleShift*, 111.

Chapter 8

A Living Record and a Well of Preaching

My (J.A.J.) friend Danny has journaled for many years, maintaining a daily habit of recording what God reveals to him through Scripture. One entire shelf of his bookcase is dedicated to his journals. He often revisits these journals. They remind him of God's faithfulness – how God has encouraged him during seasons of despair and corrected him when his attitudes or behaviors were off track. They help him recall how God gave him clarity when he wrestled with certain decisions. His journals are some of his most treasured possessions.

A Lasting Record of God's Activity in Your Life

The practice of GRIP journaling is not just a devotional tool; it is also a personal, living record of your spiritual walk. It becomes your own chronicle of divine encounters, Spirit-prompted insights, life-changing applications, and intimate conversations with God. Over time, this journal becomes a priceless legacy – a spiritual diary that testifies to how God has spoken to you through His Word so that you may live a gospel-shaped life.

Think of it this way: When you sit down with your Bible and journal, you are not merely writing reflections. You are documenting how God's unchanging Word met you in specific seasons and how the Spirit illuminated particular truths. You are recording how you chose to obey and grow.

The prophet Samuel took a stone and set it up and called its name Ebenezer, which means *Till now the* L*ORD* *has helped us* (1 Samuel 7:12). That stone was a memorial to God's faithfulness. Your GRIP journal is an Ebenezer in ink and paper.

Your journal allows you to:

- Record what you've learned about God, such as His character, His promises, and His dealings with people.
- Describe His purposes and ways and how they relate to your life.
- Trace your spiritual growth by seeing how your responses, prayers, and applications mature over time.
- Refer back for encouragement and remembrance; on dry days, you can look back and see how God previously spoke and moved.

In this way, your journal becomes a personal commentary on Scripture. You are writing what God has revealed to you. Over the years, this becomes an invaluable resource, something that future generations may read and cherish.

A Resource for Sermon Preparation

Not only is GRIP a living record of how God has shaped who you are, but it is also a source of transformational preaching.

In *Your Preaching Matters* (Aneko Press), I tell that as a young pastor I struggled to come up with sermon ideas. Sundays came fast, and I was always trying to figure out what to preach. Then I started the practice of journaling. Soon I had an unlimited supply of ideas, illustrations, and sermon material to draw from.

I once wrote a journal entry called "Removing Idols," which was based on 2 Samuel 5:21: *And the Philistines left their idols there, and David and his men carried them away.* Many months later, I was preparing a sermon on the idols in our lives that keep us from being in a right relationship with God. As I prepared my message, I remembered that I had written about idolatry in my journal, so I retrieved my journal and reread what God had revealed to me.

In the entry, I had discussed that David and his men defeated the Philistine army and burned their idols. I had also described things in my life – work, striving for success, achievements – that threatened to be idols. On the surface, such things might not appear to fall under the category of idolatry since they are seemingly innocent, but anything that becomes the greatest desire of our hearts, or anything we treasure more than God, is indeed idolatry.

The things that God had revealed to me many months prior laid the groundwork for my sermon. What is more, I was able to draw from material that had already been tried and proved in my own life. As I prepared my sermon, I knew that if I had been struggling with certain "innocent" idols, my listeners were most likely also struggling with innocent idols of their own.

For God's Word to transform your listeners, it must first transform your own life. GRIP journaling provides the means for such transformation.

For those of us who preach and teach God's Word, GRIP journaling is very beneficial. For many people in ministry, the Bible is too often approached with one dominating question: What can I preach this Sunday? Unfortunately, sermon preparation becomes the lens through which Scripture is viewed. This leads to a self-serving approach that distances the preacher's heart from God's transforming Word.

The GRIP method redirects this tendency. Instead of reading to prepare a sermon, you read to hear from God. You journal not with the goal of generating content, but with the aim of spiritual growth. It is this heart posture that leads to better sermons. Why? Because transformational preaching must first transform the preacher. As the Puritan preacher Richard Baxter said, "The Word of God must first live in the heart of the preacher before it can live in the hearts of his hearers."[32]

32 Richard Baxter, *The Reformed Pastor* (Edinburgh: Banner of Truth Trust, Edinburgh,1974), 67.

E. M. Bounds would agree. He wrote, "Preaching is not the performance of an hour. It is the outflow of a life."[33] Charles Spurgeon said it this way: "The man who is to be a preacher to others must himself first preach to himself."[34] Baxter, Bounds, and Spurgeon are saying the same thing from different angles – that what happens in the pulpit is only as deep as what has happened in the minister's devotional life. A preacher who has not been broken, searched, convicted, and comforted by the Word before Sunday morning will have very little that is truly alive to offer his people when he stands before them. The message must first pass through the messenger.

When you are personally gripped by God's Word, your preaching changes because you change. You allow the Bible to examine your own heart before you try to see how it applies to the lives of others.

A Stream That Never Runs Dry

One of the greatest challenges preachers face is the so-called dry well – the sense that they have nothing fresh to say. But when journaling using the GRIP method, you are consistently capturing God's revelation to you. Day after day and week after week, you are writing down truths, applications, and prayers that can be revisited.

This provides a wellspring of authentic sermon ideas rooted in Scripture and personal encounter. Your

33 E. M. Bounds, *Power Through Prayer* (Grand Rapids: Baker Book House, 1991), 23.

34 Charles H. Spurgeon, *Lectures to My Students* (Grand Rapids: Zondervan, 1979), 17.

biblical exposition has depth because the text has already been explored devotionally. Your illustrations spring from lived experience, and your application connects because it has been personally implemented. In this sense, GRIP transforms your journal from a personal spiritual diary into a preaching companion.

In closing, with consistent journaling you will have a record of God's faithfulness, as well as an archive of sermon ideas. When the grind of ministry tempts you to read the Word only to produce content, the GRIP method pulls you back into communion with God. Your soul is nourished, your preaching is revived, and your ministry bears fruit.

Do not allow GRIP journaling to become a rigid formula. If you just go through the motions, you will miss out on having an active conversation with the living God. But if you approach your devotions with a heart to learn, grow, and be counseled by God, you will become more like Christ day after day. And from that place of communion, you will live, serve, preach, and thrive.

Chapter 9

Counseled by God; Equipped to Counsel Others

We began this book by emphasizing that no human can counsel as God does. Every human counselor, no matter how educated or experienced, has limitations. The counselor does not know and cannot know the heart as God does. The counselor does not know one's motives as God does. And the counselor may unknowingly be blinded by his or her own subjectivity. Even though Egypt was known for its wisdom, *the wisest counselors of Pharaoh [gave] stupid counsel* (Isaiah 19:11). True wisdom comes from God.

That is why, foundationally, we need God's counsel through His Word. God's living Word faithfully guides us through life's challenges, deals with us when our thoughts are faulty, and shows us how to live Christlike lives.

While God's counsel is most faithful and reliable, He still uses human counsel – despite our limitations – to speak into the brokenness of people's lives. But if our counsel is to reflect godly wisdom, it must be grounded in God's truth. Paul David Tripp asserted, "God transforms people's lives as people bring his Word to others."[35] This transformation takes place not because of the counselor's wisdom, but because of God's. Life change becomes possible not because the counselor said the right words at the right time, but because he was a conduit to deliver God's Word at the right time.

The GRIP journaling approach helps counselors study, meditate upon, and understand and apply Scripture, making it a helpful tool in the counselor's toolbox. And when you use a Bible reading plan that guides you through all of Scripture (see Resource 3: 365-Day Bible Reading Plan), you will be grounded in the entirety of God's redemptive plan for humankind. You will have journeyed through every chapter of the Bible – even the ones you normally wouldn't read.

It is vital to know all of Scripture when giving godly counsel to others. Paul told the Ephesian elders, *I did not shrink from declaring to you the whole counsel of God* (Acts 20:27). Paul did not omit the parts of God's Word that were unpopular or that might have offended people; instead, he taught the entirety of God's Word.

This final chapter is geared for those who counsel others. The main premise of this chapter is that we can

---

35 Paul David Tripp, *Instruments in the Redeemer's Hand: People in Need of Change Helping People in Need of Change* (Phillipsburg, PA: P and R Publishing, 2002), 19.

only counsel others effectively when we have first been counseled by God.

Whether you're a pastor in a pulpit, a counselor in a session, a leader in the church, a parent at the dinner table, or a friend helping another friend who is suffering – your counsel is only as sound as your own soul is rooted in God's truth. Richard Baxter wrote, "See that the work of saving grace be thoroughly wrought in your own souls. Take heed to yourselves, lest you be void of that saving grace which you offer to others."[36]

Paul David Tripp echoed this same principle. He wrote in his book *Instruments in the Redeemer's Hand,* "Being an instrument of heart change means following Christ's example and focusing on the heart – starting with your own."[37] Before we can be used to touch another person's life with God's truth, that truth must pierce our own heart.

After my (J.A.J.) friend Rick gave his heart to Jesus, God began to shower him with peace and joy. He became eager to speak into other people's lives. Excited about all that God was doing in his own life, he was not shy about telling others how he thought they should live. His counsel, however, was not rooted in scriptural truth. He gave worldly advice based on his own experiences. Rick needed much more time in God's Word before he was equipped to counsel others. We encouraged him to share his faith with everyone, but to slow down on giving counsel until his words were shaped by scriptural truth.

36 Richard Baxter, *The Reformed Pastor* (Edinburgh: Banner of Truth Trust, 1974), 60.

37 Tripp, *Instruments*, 96.

Even longtime Christians are not equipped to counsel if they haven't been counseled by God through His Word. Going to church does not equip you. Listening to Christian podcasts does not equip you. Reading books does not equip you. Having Christian friends does not equip you. All of those things are important and beneficial, but only God equips you. A. W. Tozer warned, "It is altogether possible to run with the crowd and be carried along by the religious vogue and never have known the abiding presence of God."[38]

It is not enough to know Bible verses or have answers to people's problems. The Pharisees had knowledge, but they lacked compassion, humility, and a real relationship with God. Jesus rebuked them sharply because they taught without being transformed themselves (Matthew 23:3-4). By contrast, the best biblical counselors are those who sit daily at the feet of Jesus. They listen, learn, repent, and are healed – and then they minister out of the overflow of that healing.

Paul wrote, *Blessed be the God . . . who comforts us in all our affliction, so that we may be able to comfort those who are in any affliction* (2 Corinthians 1:3-4). Counseling begins not in a classroom but in a quiet place where God's Word counsels our hearts first.

King David is a case in point. He sinned grossly before the Lord, committing adultery with Bathsheba and orchestrating the death of her husband, Uriah the Hittite. But after the prophet Nathan confronted him, he drew near to God. He spent time in God's presence,

38 A. W. Tozer, *The Pursuit of God* (Harrisburg, PA: Christian Publications, 1948), 14.

confessing his sin and asking for forgiveness: *Wash me thoroughly from my iniquity, and cleanse me from my sin! . . . Against you, you only, have I sinned and done what is evil in your sight* (Psalm 51:2, 4).

David asked God to blot out his iniquities (v. 9) and to create in him a clean heart (v. 10). Then he said something very powerful: *Then I will teach transgressors your ways, and sinners will return to you* (v. 13). He promised to use his experience of God's grace to bring others into the knowledge of the love and grace of God. God dealt with David, and David listened, learned, and repented.

David trusted God to give him an opportunity to teach others what he had learned. That is what counseling is all about. The best counselors let God speak into their lives before they speak into the lives of others.

Become Dependent on God's Word

Men throughout the Bible demonstrated their dependence on God and His words for guidance and help. David declared that the rules of the Lord are sweeter *than honey and drippings of the honeycomb*, because *by them is your servant warned* (Psalm 19:10-11). The psalmist said, *Your testimonies are my delight; they are my counselors* (Psalm 119:24). Jeremiah said, *Your words were found, and I ate them, and your words became to me a joy and the delight of my heart* (Jeremiah 15:16). Job relied on God's counsel so much that he said, *I have treasured the words of his mouth more than my portion of food* (Job 23:12).

Jesus, however, is our greatest example of one who depended on God and His Word. For example, when tempted by Satan in the wilderness, Jesus responded to each temptation with Scripture (Matthew 4:1-11). And though He was sinless, Jesus modeled complete reliance on His Father: *I do nothing on my own authority, but speak just as the Father taught me* (John 8:28). Jesus's life was steeped in Scripture, prayer, and dependence on God.

Because of this deep communion, Jesus could speak with unmatched authority and compassion, ministering to others with truth and comforting them with grace. What a model for us to follow! Jesus depended on His Father for every aspect of His life and ministry – and so must we.

The GRIP journaling method is a spiritual lifeline that draws you into daily communion with your Counselor, Savior, and Friend. As God changes you, you become an instrument of change, taking in His counsel so that you may faithfully pass it on to others.

Using GRIP as a Counseling Tool

In chapter 7, we introduced the GRIP journaling method as an invaluable tool for discipleship and mentoring. GRIP is equally powerful in the counseling context, and we encourage you to make it a regular part of your work with counselees.

One of the most important habits you can cultivate in those you counsel is a daily engagement with Scripture. While your guidance provides structure and accountability, it is God who gives divine counsel – and lasting transformation comes when your counselees learn to hear from Him directly. No matter how skilled the counselor, there is no substitute for the living Word actively working in a person's heart and mind (Hebrews 4:12). Teaching your counselees to use GRIP gives them a framework for that daily encounter with God.

Walk them through the method carefully. Show them how to begin by reading a passage of Scripture slowly and prayerfully (God's Word), then pausing to ask what God is revealing to them through that text about Himself, about themselves, or about their situation (Revelation). From there, guide them to consider how that truth can be implemented into their lives in a concrete and specific way (Implementation), and then encourage them to respond to God in honest, personal prayer (Prayer). What makes GRIP so effective is that it moves a person from passive reading to active response.

GRIP also lends itself naturally to use as a counseling homework assignment. Between sessions, you can assign your counselees specific passages that speak directly to the issues you are addressing together. Ask them to work through each passage using GRIP and bring their journal entries to your next meeting. This keeps the counselees engaged with God's Word between appointments, reinforces what you have discussed in session, and often opens doors to deeper conversation when they return. It also gently shifts the locus of authority from the counselor to the Counselor, helping your counselees build a personal, Spirit-led practice that will sustain them long after formal counseling has ended.

In closing, we pray that GRIP will become a

meaningful part of your quiet time each day. If you miss a day, do not become discouraged; simply return to your reading plan and keep moving forward. Over time, consistency will begin to replace inconsistency, and what once felt like a discipline will become a delight. Most importantly, approach the Scriptures prayerfully, asking God to open your eyes to behold wonderful things in His Word (Psalm 119:18). When you do, you will find that GRIP will not only equip you to be Christlike, but will also give you a tool to build sermons, disciple others, and speak into their lives with the counsel you have received from God's Word.

May you be able to say along with the psalmist: *I rejoice in your word like one who discovers a great treasure* (Psalm 119:162 NLT).

Epilogue

The Power Source That Never Fails

On March 26, 2024, the 948-foot cargo ship *Dali* lost power while navigating the Patapsco River. In a matter of moments, it collided with a support pillar of the Francis Scott Key Bridge in Baltimore, causing the entire span to collapse. The world watched in horror as the infrastructure crumbled. A brief loss of power brought catastrophic destruction. Though the crew eventually restored the ship's power, it was too late. The momentum was unstoppable, and the consequence irreversible.

What happened to the Key Bridge is a vivid reminder of what can happen to our lives when we lose connection to our true power source – the Word of God. We may not feel the damage immediately. We may even regain some sense of control. But without the steady, guiding power of God's voice in our daily lives, we drift. We collide. We fall.

God's Word is a power source that never fails. It never loses connection. It is strong enough to hold you, steady enough to guide you, and clear enough to counsel you through every storm.

That is why GRIP matters. Every time you open your Bible and journal, you are plugging in to divine wisdom and divine clarity. You are being counseled by the God who spoke the world into existence – and who now speaks directly into your heart.

The difference between spiritual collapse and spiritual stability is often found in this daily connection. Do not let your life drift out of control. Be resolute about maintaining a quiet time. Keep your hand on the Word and your heart tuned to His voice every day. Keep a tight GRIP on the truth that anchors your soul.

God never stops speaking. Stay connected to Him, stay counseled by Him, and keep growing into greater Christlikeness!

Resource 1

Quick Start-Up Guide for Using GRIP

GRIP is a daily journaling method to use in your quiet time to help you hear God speak and apply His Word to your life. Use a Bible reading plan (like the ones in Resources 3-7) for your daily reading. Then structure your journal entry around four parts: (G) God's Word, (R) Revelation, (I) Implementation, and (P) Prayer.

Getting Started

Read a passage of Scripture prayerfully. Then follow these steps:

Step 1: G – Record a Verse of Scripture
Turn to a fresh page of your journal (leave the first three pages blank; they will be used for the Table of

Contents). On the left-hand side of the page, write a large "G" – this represents God's Word. Next to the G, write a verse or summary of verses that spoke to your heart from your Scripture reading.

Step 2: R – Journal What God Is Revealing

After you complete G, leave a space underneath and write a large "R," which stands for Revelation. Ask the Holy Spirit to reveal what God is saying through this passage, and write it down.

Step 3: I – Declare How You Will Obey

Once R is complete, leave a space underneath and write a large "I," which stands for Implementation. Write down how you will specifically live out this truth.

Step 4: P – Write a Prayer of Response

Now you're ready for P: Prayer. Leave a space underneath and record a personal prayer as a response to God's revelation and your implementation.

Step 5: Title Your Entry

Choose a phrase that summarizes the theme. Write the title at the top of the page. Be sure to number the page as well.

Step 6: Create a Table of Contents on Page 1

On the first page of your journal, write "Table of Contents" or "Contents" on the top center of the page. Below that, write the following headings: Title and Scripture, Date, and Page Number.

For example:

Contents

Title and Scripture	**Date**	**Page**
Fishing for Men (Mark 1:17)	1-15-25	1
What Am I Afraid Of? (Mark 4:40)	1-16-25	2
My Pain Is Gain (Genesis 50:20)	1-17-25	3

Revisit your journal entries to remind yourself of God's counsel. This method takes approximately thirty minutes a day, but will prove to be the most important part of your day.

Resource 2: Sample Journal Entries

Below are several examples of GRIP journaling. (Remember, when you create your own journal, include a Table of Contents, listing the title and Scripture passage, date, and page number. This allows you to reference your journal entries for future review.)

Walking in Boldness

G – The angel of the Lord appeared to Gideon, calling him a *mighty man of valor*. He told Gideon that the Lord was sending him to save Israel. Gideon questioned how this could be, citing his weaknesses. God assured him, *I will be with you* (Judges 6:12-16).

R – God does not see as man sees. While Gideon saw himself as weak and insignificant, God saw him through the lens of His presence and calling. The key to Gideon's success was not self-confidence, but divine partnership. God's calling redefines our identity and potential. My limitations are not liabilities when God is with me.

I – I must stop disqualifying myself based on my past or perceived inadequacies. Instead, I need to align my identity with God's Word and calling. I will approach my current responsibilities, especially those that feel beyond me, with the confidence that God has called and empowered me for them.

P – Father, I confess I often look at myself through the lens of fear and inadequacy. But You call me to see myself through Your promises and presence. Thank You that You are with me. Help me to walk in boldness and faith, knowing that my strength lies in You, not in me.

Eyes to See

G – *And let our people learn to devote themselves to good works, so as to help cases of urgent need, and not be unfruitful* (Titus 3:14).

R – Throughout chapter 3 of his letter to Titus, Paul stresses the believer's responsibility to perform good works. Our Christian call is to relieve the needs of others. When we don't, we are not bearing the fruit that God wants us to bear. Especially if there is an urgent need, we must meet it.

I – I must pay better attention to the needs around me. They're everywhere, but I get so wrapped up in my little world that I neglect to see people's hurts, struggles, and financial needs. I need to have better eyes (and a more sensitive heart) to meet the needs of others, giving my resources and talents to serve them.

P – Lord, please give me spiritual eyes to notice the needs around me. I long to be a fruit-bearing believer and to please You with my life. I surrender my selfishness and my lack of concern for others. I commit this to you in Jesus's name. Amen.

Stop Complaining

G – *How long shall this wicked congregation grumble against me? I have heard the grumblings of the people of Israel, which they grumble against me* (Numbers 14:27).

R – God hears our grumbling as a direct complaint against Him. Even our little grumblings reveal a heart that distrusts His goodness and provision. What seems like harmless complaining to me is actually a serious offense in God's sight, dishonoring His character. When I complain, it is as if I am saying, "God, you are not a good God." God desires gratitude and trust, especially in adversity.

I – I must stop justifying my complaints as harmless venting. Each time I grumble, I subtly accuse God of failing me. I will cultivate thankfulness, especially in hardship, by actively remembering and speaking of God's faithfulness. My words should reflect trust, not unbelief.

P – Forgive me, Lord, for my complaining spirit. You have been so good to me, yet I often focus on what I lack instead of praising You for all You've done. Teach me to trust You when things are hard, and let my words reflect a heart that remembers Your goodness.

God Is My Refuge

G – *God is our refuge and strength, a very present help in trouble* (Psalm 46:1).

R – God is not distant in crisis; He is present. When life is falling apart, He is near, ready to help and ready to be a refuge. He is my shelter, providing strength in any circumstance.

I – I tend to numb my anxiety with distractions and overworking. God is reminding me that He is always present, ready to be my refuge when tough times arise. When the next hardship comes, I need to come to Him and, by faith, receive the strength He provides. I cannot look to other things to comfort me or distract me.

P – Father, thank You that You are present, even when I feel alone. Help me run to You, not to worldly things that offer temporary comfort. Thank You for my strength when I am weak and for being my refuge when I feel under attack. Amen.

Confession Restores Fellowship

G – In Psalm 32:1-5, David describes the agony of unconfessed sin and the relief of being forgiven.

R – Hiding sin doesn't protect me; it robs me of peace. Confession is the pathway to peace; and more importantly, it is the pathway to restoration and intimacy with God.

I – I have been harboring bitterness toward a friend of mine because of false things he has been saying about me. I will not excuse my resentment or downplay it. I will release it. I will release it right now.

P – Merciful Father, I confess my sin of bitterness. I've let my bitterness affect my thoughts and attitudes toward my friend. I release it to You and ask You to fill me with Your peace. Forgive me, cleanse me, and restore my joy. I forgive the person who has spoken untruths about me. Please convict his heart and give me the courage to confront him in love. Thank You for Your unfailing grace! Amen.

Faith That Obeys

G – In Genesis 12, God calls Abram to leave everything familiar and go to an unknown land.

R – God is revealing the truth that faith is not theoretical, but active. Abram obeyed without knowing the outcome, simply trusting the one who called. He had courage and faith.

I – God has prompted me to start a new ministry, but I've been hesitant. I've been afraid that it won't be successful. I need to take a risk for God's kingdom and say, "Yes." If God is calling me to it, I must obey.

P – God, please give me the faith of Abraham. Help me to obey without all the answers. I trust Your promises more than my comfort. Thank You for giving me courage, strength, and wisdom. Please guide me in the next steps I should take. Amen.

Guard the Gate

G – *Keep your heart with all vigilance, for from it flow the springs of life* (Proverbs 4:23).

R – My heart is the source of my life's direction. If I'm careless with what I allow in – through media, conversations, and thoughts – it will affect everything else.

I – I feel convicted. I let so much garbage in. Garbage in, garbage out, as the saying goes. I sense that the Holy Spirit is challenging me to go on a fast from all media – music, television, entertainment, and social media. I will start today with a three-day fast and ask the Lord to show me what lasting changes I need to make to keep my heart with all vigilance. After my fast, I will commit to filtering the things I allow in my heart and mind through Philippians 4:8.

P – Lord, thank You for convicting me today. Please purify my heart. Help me to guard it with watchfulness and wisdom. As I go on this media fast, please show me lasting changes I need to make. I want to please You in every area of my life. Amen.

Being a Doer of Kindness

G – *But be doers of the word, and not hearers only, deceiving yourselves* (James 1:22).

R – Many believers read Scripture, but delay obedience or choose to not obey at all. When we are just hearers of His Word, we do not allow it to take root in our lives. What is worse, we think we are doing good because we are learning Scripture and gaining knowledge, but we are only fooling ourselves. God does not want us just to know Scripture; He wants us to obey it.

I – To be an obedient and passionate follower of Christ, I must "do" His Word. There is one particular person in my church I have little patience for, and this needs to change. The Bible says, *Love is patient and kind* (1 Corinthians 13:4), and I must become a doer of this verse.

P – Heavenly Father, please forgive me for being a "hearer" and not a "doer." "Stan" annoys me, and his know-it-all attitude about every topic drives me crazy.

Please give me patience for him. Help me to love him the same way that You love me – with patience and kindness. In Jesus's name, amen.

Humility

G – *Complete my joy by being of the same mind, having the same love, being in full accord and of one mind. Do nothing from selfish ambition or conceit, but in humility count others more significant than yourselves* (Philippians 2:2-3).

R – God's heart is for unity and humility in His people. Selfishness, pride, and personal agendas destroy the unity Christ died to create. True Christlikeness is seen in considering others as more important than ourselves. The church thrives when love and humility replace ambition and ego.

I – In my relationships, I will intentionally honor others, listen more than I speak, and seek their good above my own. This applies especially in my relationships with my family and church family; my attitude must reflect Christ's humility. I am a servant.

P – Jesus, humble King, thank You for demonstrating what it means to put others first. Help me to die to selfish ambition and pride. Teach me to walk in true humility and love, especially with those closest to me. Make me an instrument of unity in my home and my church. Amen.

Obedience over Comfort

G – *By faith Moses, when he was grown up, refused to be called the son of Pharaoh's daughter, choosing rather to be mistreated with the people of God. . . , for he considered the reproach of Christ greater wealth than the treasures of Egypt, for he was looking to the reward* (Hebrews 11:24-26).

R – Faith makes us choose eternal reward over temporary comfort. Moses could have lived a life of luxury, but he chose obedience, even though it meant suffering. He valued God's approval above Egypt's riches. This reveals God's call to live with an eternal perspective and embrace the cost of following Him.

I – I must stop seeking security and comfort as my highest goals. I will make choices based on eternal value, not earthly success. I will embrace discomfort, loss, or rejection if it means obeying Christ. Like Moses, I will keep my eyes on the reward that only God can give.

P – Lord, I confess that I often choose what is easy over what is right. Give me the faith of Moses – to reject the treasures of this world in favor of Your reward. Help me to suffer well for Your name, knowing that obedience to You is worth everything. Amen.

Resource 3

365-Day Bible Reading Plan

This reading plan allows you to read through the entire Bible in one year and the New Testament twice. Each day includes a passage from the Old Testament and one or more chapters from the New Testament, keeping Christ central to your daily walk with God.

Date	**Old Testament Reading**	**New Testament Reading**
Jan 01	Genesis 1-3	Matthew 1-2
Jan 02	Genesis 4-6	Matthew 3-4
Jan 03	Genesis 7-9	Matthew 5-6
Jan 04	Genesis 10-12	Matthew 7-8
Jan 05	Genesis 13-15	Matthew 9-10
Jan 06	Genesis 16-18	Matthew 11-12
Jan 07	Genesis 19-21	Matthew 13-14

Jan 08	Genesis 22-24	Matthew 15-16
Jan 09	Genesis 25-27	Matthew 17-18
Jan 10	Genesis 28-30	Matthew 19-20
Jan 11	Genesis 31-33	Matthew 21-22
Jan 12	Genesis 34-36	Matthew 23-24
Jan 13	Genesis 37-39	Matthew 25-26
Jan 14	Genesis 40-42	Matthew 27-28
Jan 15	Genesis 43-45	Mark 1-2
Jan 16	Genesis 46-48	Mark 3-4
Jan 17	Genesis 49-50; Exodus 1	Mark 5-6
Jan 18	Exodus 2-4	Mark 7-8
Jan 19	Exodus 5-7	Mark 9-10
Jan 20	Exodus 8-10	Mark 11-12
Jan 21	Exodus 11-13	Mark 13-14
Jan 22	Exodus 14-16	Mark 15-16
Jan 23	Exodus 17-19	Luke 1-2
Jan 24	Exodus 20-22	Luke 3-4
Jan 25	Exodus 23-25	Luke 5-6
Jan 26	Exodus 26-28	Luke 7-8
Jan 27	Exodus 29-31	Luke 9-10
Jan 28	Exodus 32-34	Luke 11-12
Jan 29	Exodus 35-37	Luke 13-14
Jan 30	Exodus 38-40	Luke 15-16
Jan 31	Leviticus 1-3	Luke 17-18
Feb 01	Leviticus 4-6	Luke 19-20
Feb 02	Leviticus 7-9	Luke 21-22
Feb 03	Leviticus 10-12	Luke 23-24
Feb 04	Leviticus 13-15	John 1-2
Feb 05	Leviticus 16-18	John 3-4

Feb 06	Leviticus 19-21	John 5-6
Feb 07	Leviticus 22-24	John 7-8
Feb 08	Leviticus 25-27	John 9-10
Feb 09	Numbers 1-3	John 11-12
Feb 10	Numbers 4-6	John 13-14
Feb 11	Numbers 7-9	John 15-16
Feb 12	Numbers 10-12	John 17-18
Feb 13	Numbers 13-15	John 19-20
Feb 14	Numbers 16-18	John 21; Acts 1
Feb 15	Numbers 19-21	Acts 2-3
Feb 16	Numbers 22-24	Acts 4-5
Feb 17	Numbers 25-27	Acts 6-7
Feb 18	Numbers 28-30	Acts 8-9
Feb 19	Numbers 31-33	Acts 10-11
Feb 20	Numbers 34-36	Acts 12-13
Feb 21	Deuteronomy 1-3	Acts 14-15
Feb 22	Deuteronomy 4-6	Acts 16-17
Feb 23	Deuteronomy 7-9	Acts 18-19
Feb 24	Deuteronomy 10-12	Acts 20-21
Feb 25	Deuteronomy 13-15	Acts 22-23
Feb 26	Deuteronomy 16-18	Acts 24-25
Feb 27	Deuteronomy 19-21	Acts 26-27
Feb 28	Deuteronomy 22-24	Acts 28; Romans 1
Mar 01	Deuteronomy 25-27	Romans 2-3
Mar 02	Deuteronomy 28-30	Romans 4-5
Mar 03	Deuteronomy 31-33	Romans 6-7
Mar 04	Deuteronomy 34; Joshua 1-2	Romans 8-9
Mar 05	Joshua 3-5	Romans 10-11
Mar 06	Joshua 6-8	Romans 12-13

Mar 07	Joshua 9-11	Romans 14-15
Mar 08	Joshua 12-14	Romans 16; 1 Corinthians 1
Mar 09	Joshua 15-17	1 Corinthians 2-3
Mar 10	Joshua 18-20	1 Corinthians 4-5
Mar 11	Joshua 21-23	1 Corinthians 6-7
Mar 12	Joshua 24; Judges 1-2	1 Corinthians 8-9
Mar 13	Judges 3-5	1 Corinthians 10-11
Mar 14	Judges 6-8	1 Corinthians 12-13
Mar 15	Judges 9-11	1 Corinthians 14-15
Mar 16	Judges 12-14	1 Corinthians 16; 2 Corinthians 1
Mar 17	Judges 15-17	2 Corinthians 2-3
Mar 18	Judges 18-20	2 Corinthians 4-5
Mar 19	Judges 21; Ruth 1-2	2 Corinthians 6-7
Mar 20	Ruth 3-4; 1 Samuel 1	2 Corinthians 8-9
Mar 21	1 Samuel 2-4	2 Corinthians 10-11
Mar 22	1 Samuel 5-7	2 Corinthians 12-13
Mar 23	1 Samuel 8-10	Galatians 1-2
Mar 24	1 Samuel 11-13	Galatians 3-4
Mar 25	1 Samuel 14-16	Galatians 5-6
Mar 26	1 Samuel 17-19	Ephesians 1-2
Mar 27	1 Samuel 20-22	Ephesians 3-4
Mar 28	1 Samuel 23-25	Ephesians 5-6
Mar 29	1 Samuel 26-28	Philippians 1-2
Mar 30	1 Samuel 29-31	Philippians 3-4
Mar 31	2 Samuel 1-3	Colossians 1-2
Apr 01	2 Samuel 4-6	Colossians 3-4
Apr 02	2 Samuel 7-9	1 Thessalonians 1-2
Apr 03	2 Samuel 10-12	1 Thessalonians 3-4

Apr 04	2 Samuel 13-15	1 Thessalonians 5; 2 Thessalonians 1
Apr 05	2 Samuel 16-18	2 Thessalonians 2-3
Apr 06	2 Samuel 19-21	1 Timothy 1-2
Apr 07	2 Samuel 22-24	1 Timothy 3-4
Apr 08	1 Kings 1-3	1 Timothy 5-6
Apr 09	1 Kings 4-6	2 Timothy 1-2
Apr 10	1 Kings 7-9	2 Timothy 3-4
Apr 11	1 Kings 10-12	Titus 1-2
Apr 12	1 Kings 13-15	Titus 3; Philemon 1
Apr 13	1 Kings 16-18	Hebrews 1-2
Apr 14	1 Kings 19-21	Hebrews 3-4
Apr 15	1 Kings 22; 2 Kings 1-2	Hebrews 5-6
Apr 16	2 Kings 3-5	Hebrews 7-8
Apr 17	2 Kings 6-8	Hebrews 9-10
Apr 18	2 Kings 9-11	Hebrews 11-12
Apr 19	2 Kings 12-14	Hebrews 13; James 1
Apr 20	2 Kings 15-17	James 2-3
Apr 21	2 Kings 18-20	James 4-5
Apr 22	2 Kings 21-23	1 Peter 1-2
Apr 23	2 Kings 24-25; 1 Chronicles 1	1 Peter 3-4
Apr 24	1 Chronicles 2-4	1 Peter 5; 2 Peter 1
Apr 25	1 Chronicles 5-7	2 Peter 2-3
Apr 26	1 Chronicles 8-10	1 John 1-2
Apr 27	1 Chronicles 11-13	1 John 3-4
Apr 28	1 Chronicles 14-16	1 John 5; 2 John 1
Apr 29	1 Chronicles 17-19	3 John 1; Jude 1
Apr 30	1 Chronicles 20-22	Revelation 1-2

May 01	1 Chronicles 23-25	Revelation 3-4
May 02	1 Chronicles 26-28	Revelation 5-6
May 03	1 Chronicles 29; 2 Chronicles 1-2	Revelation 7-8
May 04	2 Chronicles 3-5	Revelation 9-10
May 05	2 Chronicles 6-8	Revelation 11-12
May 06	2 Chronicles 9-11	Revelation 13-14
May 07	2 Chronicles 12-14	Revelation 15-16
May 08	2 Chronicles 15-17	Revelation 17-18
May 09	2 Chronicles 18-20	Revelation 19-20
May 10	2 Chronicles 21-23	Revelation 21-22
May 11	2 Chronicles 24-26	Matthew 1-2
May 12	2 Chronicles 27-29	Matthew 3-4
May 13	2 Chronicles 30-32	Matthew 5-6
May 14	2 Chronicles 33-35	Matthew 7-8
May 15	2 Chronicles 36; Ezra 1-2	Matthew 9-10
May 16	Ezra 3-5	Matthew 11-12
May 17	Ezra 6-8	Matthew 13-14
May 18	Ezra 9-10; Nehemiah 1	Matthew 15-16
May 19	Nehemiah 2-4	Matthew 17-18
May 20	Nehemiah 5-7	Matthew 19-20
May 21	Nehemiah 8-10	Matthew 21-22
May 22	Nehemiah 11-13	Matthew 23-24
May 23	Esther 1-3	Matthew 25-26
May 24	Esther 4-6	Matthew 27-28
May 25	Esther 7-9	Mark 1-2
May 26	Esther 10; Job 1-2	Mark 3-4
May 27	Job 3-5	Mark 5-6
May 28	Job 6-8	Mark 7-8
May 29	Job 9-11	Mark 9-10

May 30	Job 12-14	Mark 11-12
May 31	Job 15-17	Mark 13-14
Jun 01	Job 18-20	Mark 15-16
Jun 02	Job 21-23	Luke 1-2
Jun 03	Job 24-26	Luke 3-4
Jun 04	Job 27-29	Luke 5-6
Jun 05	Job 30-32	Luke 7
Jun 06	Job 33-35	Luke 8
Jun 07	Job 36-38	Luke 9
Jun 08	Job 39-41	Luke 10
Jun 09	Job 42; Psalms 1-2	Luke 11
Jun 10	Psalms 3-5	Luke 12
Jun 11	Psalms 6-8	Luke 13
Jun 12	Psalms 9-11	Luke 14
Jun 13	Psalms 12-14	Luke 15
Jun 14	Psalms 15-17	Luke 16
Jun 15	Psalms 18-20	Luke 17
Jun 16	Psalms 21-23	Luke 18
Jun 17	Psalms 24-26	Luke 19
Jun 18	Psalms 27-29	Luke 20
Jun 19	Psalms 30-32	Luke 21
Jun 20	Psalms 33-35	Luke 22
Jun 21	Psalms 36-38	Luke 23
Jun 22	Psalms 39-41	Luke 24
Jun 23	Psalms 42-44	John 1
Jun 24	Psalms 45-47	John 2
Jun 25	Psalms 48-50	John 3
Jun 26	Psalms 51-53	John 4
Jun 27	Psalms 54-56	John 5
Jun 28	Psalms 57-59	John 6

Jun 29	Psalms 60-62	John 7
Jun 30	Psalms 63-65	John 8
Jul 01	Psalms 66-68	John 9
Jul 02	Psalms 69-71	John 10
Jul 03	Psalms 72-74	John 11
Jul 04	Psalms 75-77	John 12
Jul 05	Psalms 78-80	John 13
Jul 06	Psalms 81-83	John 14
Jul 07	Psalms 84-86	John 15
Jul 08	Psalms 87-89	John 16
Jul 09	Psalms 90-92	John 17
Jul 10	Psalms 93-95	John 18
Jul 11	Psalms 96-98	John 19
Jul 12	Psalms 99-101	John 20
Jul 13	Psalms 102-104	John 21
Jul 14	Psalms 105-107	Acts 1
Jul 15	Psalms 108-110	Acts 2
Jul 16	Psalms 111-113	Acts 3
Jul 17	Psalms 114-116	Acts 4
Jul 18	Psalms 117-119	Acts 5
Jul 19	Psalms 120-121	Acts 6
Jul 20	Psalms 122-123	Acts 7
Jul 21	Psalms 124-125	Acts 8
Jul 22	Psalms 126-127	Acts 9
Jul 23	Psalms 128-129	Acts 10
Jul 24	Psalms 130-131	Acts 11
Jul 25	Psalms 132-133	Acts 12
Jul 26	Psalms 134-135	Acts 13
Jul 27	Psalms 136-137	Acts 14
Jul 28	Psalms 138-139	Acts 15

Jul 29	Psalms 140-141	Acts 16
Jul 30	Psalms 142-143	Acts 17
Jul 31	Psalms 144-145	Acts 18
Aug 01	Psalms 146-147	Acts 19
Aug 02	Psalms 148-149	Acts 20
Aug 03	Psalms 150; Proverbs 1	Acts 21
Aug 04	Proverbs 2-3	Acts 22
Aug 05	Proverbs 4-5	Acts 23
Aug 06	Proverbs 6-7	Acts 24
Aug 07	Proverbs 8-9	Acts 25
Aug 08	Proverbs 10-11	Acts 26
Aug 09	Proverbs 12-13	Acts 27
Aug 10	Proverbs 14-15	Acts 28
Aug 11	Proverbs 16-17	Romans 1
Aug 12	Proverbs 18-19	Romans 2
Aug 13	Proverbs 20-21	Romans 3
Aug 14	Proverbs 22-23	Romans 4
Aug 15	Proverbs 24-25	Romans 5
Aug 16	Proverbs 26-27	Romans 6
Aug 17	Proverbs 28-29	Romans 7
Aug 18	Proverbs 30-31	Romans 8
Aug 19	Ecclesiastes 1-2	Romans 9
Aug 20	Ecclesiastes 3-4	Romans 10
Aug 21	Ecclesiastes 5-6	Romans 11
Aug 22	Ecclesiastes 7-8	Romans 12
Aug 23	Ecclesiastes 9-10	Romans 13
Aug 24	Ecclesiastes 11-12	Romans 14
Aug 25	Song of Solomon 1-2	Romans 15
Aug 26	Song of Solomon 3-4	Romans 16
Aug 27	Song of Solomon 5-6	1 Corinthians 1

Aug 28	Song of Solomon 7-8	1 Corinthians 2
Aug 29	Isaiah 1-2	1 Corinthians 3
Aug 30	Isaiah 3-4	1 Corinthians 4
Aug 31	Isaiah 5-6	1 Corinthians 5
Sep 01	Isaiah 7-8	1 Corinthians 6
Sep 02	Isaiah 9-10	1 Corinthians 7
Sep 03	Isaiah 11-12	1 Corinthians 8
Sep 04	Isaiah 13-14	1 Corinthians 9
Sep 05	Isaiah 15-16	1 Corinthians 10
Sep 06	Isaiah 17-18	1 Corinthians 11
Sep 07	Isaiah 19-20	1 Corinthians 12
Sep 08	Isaiah 21-22	1 Corinthians 13
Sep 09	Isaiah 23-24	1 Corinthians 14
Sep 10	Isaiah 25-26	1 Corinthians 15
Sep 11	Isaiah 27-28	1 Corinthians 16
Sep 12	Isaiah 29-30	2 Corinthians 1
Sep 13	Isaiah 31-32	2 Corinthians 2
Sep 14	Isaiah 33-34	2 Corinthians 3
Sep 15	Isaiah 35-36	2 Corinthians 4
Sep 16	Isaiah 37-38	2 Corinthians 5
Sep 17	Isaiah 39-40	2 Corinthians 6
Sep 18	Isaiah 41-42	2 Corinthians 7
Sep 19	Isaiah 43-44	2 Corinthians 8
Sep 20	Isaiah 45-46	2 Corinthians 9
Sep 21	Isaiah 47-48	2 Corinthians 10
Sep 22	Isaiah 49-50	2 Corinthians 11
Sep 23	Isaiah 51-52	2 Corinthians 12
Sep 24	Isaiah 53-54	2 Corinthians 13
Sep 25	Isaiah 55-56	Galatians 1
Sep 26	Isaiah 57-58	Galatians 2

Sep 27	Isaiah 59-60	Galatians 3
Sep 28	Isaiah 61-62	Galatians 4
Sep 29	Isaiah 63-64	Galatians 5
Sep 30	Isaiah 65-66	Galatians 6
Oct 01	Jeremiah 1-2	Ephesians 1
Oct 02	Jeremiah 3-4	Ephesians 2
Oct 03	Jeremiah 5-6	Ephesians 3
Oct 04	Jeremiah 7-8	Ephesians 4
Oct 05	Jeremiah 9-10	Ephesians 5
Oct 06	Jeremiah 11-12	Ephesians 6
Oct 07	Jeremiah 13-14	Philippians 1
Oct 08	Jeremiah 15-16	Philippians 2
Oct 09	Jeremiah 17-18	Philippians 3
Oct 10	Jeremiah 19-20	Philippians 4
Oct 11	Jeremiah 21-22	Colossians 1
Oct 12	Jeremiah 23-24	Colossians 2
Oct 13	Jeremiah 25-26	Colossians 3
Oct 14	Jeremiah 27-28	Colossians 4
Oct 15	Jeremiah 29-30	1 Thessalonians 1
Oct 16	Jeremiah 31-32	1 Thessalonians 2
Oct 17	Jeremiah 33-34	1 Thessalonians 3
Oct 18	Jeremiah 35-36	1 Thessalonians 4
Oct 19	Jeremiah 37-38	1 Thessalonians 5
Oct 20	Jeremiah 39-40	2 Thessalonians 1
Oct 21	Jeremiah 41-42	2 Thessalonians 2
Oct 22	Jeremiah 43-44	2 Thessalonians 3
Oct 23	Jeremiah 45-46	1 Timothy 1
Oct 24	Jeremiah 47-48	1 Timothy 2
Oct 25	Jeremiah 49-50	1 Timothy 3
Oct 26	Jeremiah 51-52	1 Timothy 4

Oct 27	Lamentations 1-2	1 Timothy 5
Oct 28	Lamentations 3-4	1 Timothy 6
Oct 29	Lamentations 5; Ezekiel 1	2 Timothy 1
Oct 30	Ezekiel 2-3	2 Timothy 2
Oct 31	Ezekiel 4-5	2 Timothy 3
Nov 01	Ezekiel 6-7	2 Timothy 4
Nov 02	Ezekiel 8-9	Titus 1
Nov 03	Ezekiel 10-11	Titus 2
Nov 04	Ezekiel 12-13	Titus 3
Nov 05	Ezekiel 14-15	Philemon 1
Nov 06	Ezekiel 16-17	Hebrews 1
Nov 07	Ezekiel 18-19	Hebrews 2
Nov 08	Ezekiel 20-21	Hebrews 3
Nov 09	Ezekiel 22-23	Hebrews 4
Nov 10	Ezekiel 24-25	Hebrews 5
Nov 11	Ezekiel 26-27	Hebrews 6
Nov 12	Ezekiel 28-29	Hebrews 7
Nov 13	Ezekiel 30-31	Hebrews 8
Nov 14	Ezekiel 32-33	Hebrews 9
Nov 15	Ezekiel 34-35	Hebrews 10
Nov 16	Ezekiel 36-37	Hebrews 11
Nov 17	Ezekiel 38-39	Hebrews 12
Nov 18	Ezekiel 40-41	Hebrews 13
Nov 19	Ezekiel 42-43	James 1
Nov 20	Ezekiel 44-45	James 2
Nov 21	Ezekiel 46-47	James 3
Nov 22	Ezekiel 48; Daniel 1	James 4
Nov 23	Daniel 2-3	James 5
Nov 24	Daniel 4-5	1 Peter 1

Nov 25	Daniel 6-7	1 Peter 2
Nov 26	Daniel 8-9	1 Peter 3
Nov 27	Daniel 10-11	1 Peter 4
Nov 28	Daniel 12; Hosea 1	1 Peter 5
Nov 29	Hosea 2-3	2 Peter 1
Nov 30	Hosea 4-5	2 Peter 2
Dec 01	Hosea 6-7	2 Peter 3
Dec 02	Hosea 8-9	1 John 1
Dec 03	Hosea 10-11	1 John 2
Dec 04	Hosea 12-13	1 John 3
Dec 05	Hosea 14; Joel 1	1 John 4
Dec 06	Joel 2-3	1 John 5
Dec 07	Amos 1-2	2 John 1
Dec 08	Amos 3-4	3 John 1
Dec 09	Amos 5-6	Jude 1
Dec 10	Amos 7-8	Revelation 1
Dec 11	Amos 9; Obadiah 1	Revelation 2
Dec 12	Jonah 1-2	Revelation 3
Dec 13	Jonah 3-4	Revelation 4
Dec 14	Micah 1-2	Revelation 5
Dec 15	Micah 3-4	Revelation 6
Dec 16	Micah 5-6	Revelation 7
Dec 17	Micah 7; Nahum 1	Revelation 8
Dec 18	Nahum 2-3	Revelation 9
Dec 19	Habakkuk 1-2	Revelation 10
Dec 20	Habakkuk 3; Zephaniah 1	Revelation 11
Dec 21	Zephaniah 2-3	Revelation 12
Dec 22	Haggai 1-2	Revelation 13
Dec 23	Zechariah 1-2	Revelation 14

Dec 24	Zechariah 3-4	Revelation 15
Dec 25	Zechariah 5-6	Revelation 16
Dec 26	Zechariah 7-8	Revelation 17
Dec 27	Zechariah 9-10	Revelation 18
Dec 28	Zechariah 11-12	Revelation 19
Dec 29	Zechariah 13-14	Revelation 20
Dec 30	Malachi 1-2	Revelation 21
Dec 31	Malachi 3-4	Revelation 22

Resource 4

30-Day Reading Plan for Spiritual Growth

This plan will help you mature in your walk with God, focusing on identity in Christ, obedience, prayer, and transformation.

Day	Scripture
1	John 15, Galatians 5
2	Romans 6, 8
3	Ephesians 1-2
4	Colossians 1, 3
5	Psalm 1, 19
6	James 1-2
7	2 Peter 1, 3
8	1 John 1-2
9	Philippians 1-2
10	Matthew 5-6
11	Proverbs 3-4

Day	Scripture
12	Psalms 23, 139
13	Romans 12, 14
14	Hebrews 12-13
15	Isaiah 40, 55
16	John 3, 10
17	Matthew 11, 16
18	Psalms 27, 34
19	Luke 9, 14
20	Titus 2-3
21	Acts 2, 4
22	1 Corinthians 2, 13
23	Galatians 2, 6
24	Ephesians 3-4
25	Job 1-2
26	Revelation 2-3
27	Zechariah 4; Micah 6
28	Lamentations 3; Psalm 51
29	Matthew 7, 25
30	Romans 5; John 17

Resource 5

30-Day Reading Plan for Leadership Development

Designed to build character and conviction in Christian leaders, this plan emphasizes integrity, vision, courage, and servant leadership.

Day	Scripture
1	Nehemiah 1-2
2	Nehemiah 3-4
3	Nehemiah 5-6
4	Exodus 18; Deuteronomy 1
5	1 Timothy 3; Titus 1
6	Acts 6, 20
7	Matthew 20; John 13
8	Proverbs 16, 22
9	Joshua 1-2
10	Joshua 3-4
11	Judges 4-5

Day	Scripture
12	1 Samuel 16-17
13	1 Samuel 18, 20
14	2 Samuel 5; Psalm 78
15	2 Kings 18-19
16	Daniel 1-2
17	Daniel 3-4
18	Isaiah 6; Jeremiah 1
19	Matthew 5-6
20	Luke 22; John 21
21	2 Corinthians 4-5
22	Galatians 1-2
23	1 Thessalonians 2; 1 Peter 5
24	Hebrews 13; James 3
25	Exodus 33-34
26	Psalms 101, 112
27	Romans 12-13
28	2 Timothy 1-2
29	Revelation 2-3
30	Revelation 4-5

Resource 6

30-Day Reading Plan for Walking in the Promises of God

This plan anchors you in the promises of God so that you may walk confidently, no matter what you face.

Day	Scripture
1	Genesis 12, 15
2	Genesis 17, 22
3	Exodus 3, 6
4	Deuteronomy 28, 30
5	Joshua 1, 23
6	2 Samuel 7; Psalm 89
7	1 Kings 8-9
8	Isaiah 40-41
9	Isaiah 43, 55
10	Jeremiah 29, 31

Day	Scripture
11	Ezekiel 36-37
12	Zechariah 8, 10
13	Matthew 6-7
14	Matthew 11, 28
15	Luke 1, 4
16	John 10, 14
17	John 15-16
18	Acts 1-2
19	Acts 3-4
20	Romans 4, 8
21	2 Corinthians 1, 4
22	Galatians 3, 5
23	Ephesians 1-2
24	Philippians 4; Colossians 1
25	2 Thessalonians 2; 2 Timothy 1
26	Hebrews 6, 11
27	Hebrews 12; James 1
28	1 Peter 1, 5
29	2 Peter 1, 3
30	Revelation 21-22

Resource 7

30-Day Reading Plan for Victory over the Enemy

This plan equips you with God's truth to resist the devil, overcome temptation, and walk in daily victory.

Day	Scripture
1	Genesis 3; Romans 5
2	Exodus 14; Psalm 91
3	Joshua 6, 10
4	Judges 7, 16
5	1 Samuel 17; 1 Kings 18
6	Job 12
7	Psalms 18, 27
8	Psalms 34, 46
9	Psalm 144; Isaiah 54
10	Isaiah 59, 61
11	Matthew 4, 8

Day	Scripture
12	Matthew 10, 12
13	Matthew 16-17
14	Luke 4, 10
15	John 8, 16
16	Acts 8, 16
17	Romans 6, 8
18	Romans 13; 1 Corinthians 10
19	2 Corinthians 10; Galatians 5
20	Ephesians 4, 6
21	Philippians 2, 4
22	Colossians 2-3
23	1 Thessalonians 5; 2 Thessalonians 3
24	1 Timothy 6; 2 Timothy 2
25	2 Timothy 3-4
26	Hebrews 2, 4
27	Hebrews 10, 12
28	James 1, 4
29	1 Peter 5; 1 John 4
30	Revelation 12, 20

Resource 8

GRIP Starter Journal

You will need a composition book or a blank journal to begin GRIP journaling. If you do not have one yet, use the Starter Journal on the following pages to get started today.

Table of Contents

*Title and Scripture*____________ *Date*________ *Page*____

Journal Title

Journal Title

Journal Title

Journal Title

Journal Title

Journal Title

Journal Title

Journal Title

Journal Title

Journal Title

Acknowledgements

I would like to acknowledge the efforts of those who made invaluable contributions to this project. It takes many people to write a book, and I appreciate the efforts of everyone who donated their time and talents. Dawn Little helped organize the first draft, making sure everything was formatted correctly. David Johnson invested much time in research, sources, and other support. B. Woolsey helped me fix clumsy sentences. P. Sanchez helped with copyedits and overall flow. And Judy "The Closer" Fry ensured that the manuscript was ready for submission. Thank you all so much for your continued dedication to help others experience life transformation through the power of the gospel.

About the Authors

David N. Johnson

David was born and raised in California, where he met and married his childhood sweetheart, Lisa, in 1986. Together they have built a rich family life, now graced with three daughters and nine grandchildren who are the joy of their lives. David and Lisa divide their time between homes in Texas and Arizona, and they love to travel – especially to visit their children and grandchildren scattered across the country.

David has devoted his career to two parallel callings: serving people's financial futures and serving the church. He has been a wealth manager since 1990 and founded Johnson Wealth Management, an investment advisory firm, in 1994. He holds multiple financial designations and has spent more than three decades helping individuals, families, businesses, and charities pursue financial clarity and confidence.

At the same time, David has served the body of Christ as an ordained minister, church planter, and elder, drawing on nearly thirty years of pastoral experience. He currently serves as president of Genesis College and Seminary, and serves on several boards and foundations, lending his leadership to causes that reflect his conviction that the gospel transforms every dimension of human life. David is the author and coauthor of several books, including *Investing Wisely* and *How to Start a House Church Anywhere*, and served as editor of *What's Great About God*.

J. A. Johnson

Dr. Johnson is a founding member of Genesis College and Seminary, a Christian institution committed to providing biblical higher education to incarcerated men and women through distance-based learning. In addition to the academic materials and leadership courses he has designed for Genesis, Johnson has coauthored several books, including *Your Character Matters*, *Your Preaching Matters*, *Investing Wisely*, and *How to Start a House Church Anywhere*.

Johnson is an ordained minister and has served as the senior pastor of churches in both California and Arizona. He has also served as an adjunct professor at several Christian universities. The dissertation for his PhD is a seminal work in the field of volunteer motivation. Building on his research, researchers and scholars quote him and his work in several academic journals, including *Voluntas*, the journal of Johns Hopkins University. Johnson adores his four children and seven grandchildren.

www.ingramcontent.com/pod-product-compliance
Lightning Source LLC
LaVergne TN
LVHW010605160826
845677LV00013B/3251

* 9 7 9 8 8 8 9 3 6 5 8 0 8 *